Liz Martin

STILL STANDING
An Irishwoman's Story of HIV and Hope

D1340325

Still Standing is a work of non-fiction based on the life of the author. All names have been changed to protect the privacy of others. The author has warranted to the publisher that the contents are true. While the publisher has taken care to explore and check where reasonably possible, they have not verified all the information in this book and do not warrant its veracity in all respects.

First published in 2007 by AIDS West

AIDS West
Ozanam House
St. Augustine St.
Galway
Ireland
Phone: 353 91 566266
Fax: 353 91 564708
Email: info@aidswest.ie
www.aidswest.ie

ISBN 978–0–9555884–0–2, *paperback*

Editor: Geraldine Mills
Printing: Betaprint, Dublin
Cover design: Clifford Hayes

FOREWORD

As a writer I am constantly drawn to the power of story, whether it is the narrative behind a painting, a poem or a piece of sculpture. That is why when AIDS West asked me in 2005 to read the opening chapters of a memoir by one of its clients to view it for publication, I knew immediately that this was a project I wanted to be part of.

Liz Martin started writing her life story about 10 years previously, but it got lost somewhere within the turmoil of her existence, and now here was an opportunity to support her in finishing it. It is no exaggeration to say that Liz has had a turbulent life, but turbulence alone doesn't make good memoir. What made me want to see this book to fruition was the way she documented her journey – much of it very harrowing – with such honesty and bravery in a true and totally unsentimental style which I was certain would capture the most reluctant of readers.

And so we worked together, long conversations on the phone about certain passages and the eagerly awaited envelope of now familiar handwriting. There were the trips eastwards to spend afternoons in the Gresham and Wynnes; while coffees went cold we teased out what episode should come next, or walked the length of O'Connell St. listing out possible titles to one another. One chapter of her brave journey followed another, and now it is in print.

To say it has been a privilege to work with someone as courageous and determined as Liz is an understatement. When she was first diagnosed with HIV, she would have given anything to have been able to get her hands on the story of someone with the virus living in Ireland. Sixteen years on, her story has a greater resonance for those who have been newly diagnosed. She clearly shows that it is possible to a live a long and healthy life with the virus. She has survived on her own triple therapy of medical treatments, laughter and hope – and the greatest of these is hope. Thank you Liz for trusting me with your life experience. I salute your enormous courage in putting your name to *Still Standing*.

Geraldine Mills

Acknowledgements

This book is dedicated to my children, without whom I wouldn't be here. You gave me hope when I had none, a reason to live when there wasn't any, the strength to get out of bed in the mornings and the courage to stand up in the face of adversity and take on the world. I love you now and forever.

To my best friends Alison and Cathy and your families, thank you for being there for me when I needed you most. You have helped pick up the pieces of my shattered life over many years.

To the angels I have met along the way, you know who you are. I thank you most sincerely for opening your hearts and doors and giving me much needed support.

To Martin, it was an honour to have met you and have you in my life.

To the medical staff of Beaumont Hospital, thank you for your care.

And finally to all those who have worked for AIDS West Galway over the years; you've made the world a better place. It's hard to thank you all individually so heartfelt thanks to those of you who still remember me. To Ev, Maudie, Gerry, Nick, Colm, Kieran, Sharon and Rosaleen, thanks for the encouragement and the work you've all done. I am very grateful to the manager of AIDS West, Orla Nugent Irwin, and the board of directors of AIDS West without whose support the book would not have been written.

To Geraldine who has been my inspiration and has worked tirelessly, helping me to put this book together over the last two years. I solemnly thank you for believing that I had the potential to write.

To My Children

God grant me the serenity
to accept the things I cannot change
the courage to change the things I can
and the wisdom to know the difference

STILL STANDING

CHAPTER 1

My story begins back in 1967, that's the year I was born. My family lived in the Liberties, the oldest part of Dublin. It's here they say the real Dubliners come from, the old stock. My father worked in Urneys, the sweet factory. My mother stayed at home and looked after my sister, Sandra and my two brothers, Davy and Tommy, and of course me. My name is Anna, Anna Mahon.

When I was only six weeks old the tenement building we lived in was earmarked for demolition and we had to move out. My parents were given the option of a house on Dublin's northside or a flat in an inner city complex. Without any discussion, my father made the decision and signed for the key to our new home. We moved into the flat the next day.

The flats' complex was newly built and consisted of three blocks, with ten families on each landing. The entrance to each landing was through a flight of concrete stairs encased in a grey tower with wire-meshed windows. Disposal of rubbish was done through a chute at the end of each landing. St. Stephen's Green and Patrick's Park were our back gardens and that's where we spent our days as we grew. Many an hour we whiled away there, playing ball and feeding the ducks – if there were any stale scraps of bread left over at home. We chased each other and collected the chestnuts that fell from the trees in autumn, running home before dark with our pockets full of conkers.

My mother had barely finished unpacking the few possessions we had when my father came home and told her the factory had made him redundant. This was another big blow for the family. With my father out of a job and little money coming into the house, raising four young children would be a mammoth task for her. Poverty and unemployment were widespread, and we were no exception to that. This was inner city Dublin of the late sixties. The little she did have was shared among us, and we were reared to have great respect and appreciation for everything that was given to us.

Money was so scarce my mother couldn't afford a pram, and I was carried everywhere as a baby. When I did start walking, I was brought by the hand over to Halligan's Bakery at the end of Oliver Bond Hill, for the cheap bread. As I grew older, my father still showed no signs of getting work, and each year my mother struggled to make ends meet. That task became even harder for her when, like many men in the area, he took to the drink.

I started school at a local convent in the Coombe. I remember with fondness the bread and jam sandwiches and the free milk. I was the only one who could count from one to ten in Irish, and Sister Rose loved me for it.

I had great interest in school which my father often resented. 'Ignorance and education go hand in hand, in my book. Don't you forget that,' he used to say to me, words I still remember to this day.

My sister Sandra, who is 12 years older than me, went to London to work as a chambermaid in Shepherd's Bush. By the time it came for me to make my First Holy Communion, my dress was bought with the few bob she sent home. It was 1974, CIE had gone on strike, bombs were going off around the city and Rolf Harris cried when he sang *Two Little Boys* on the *Late Late Show*. Getting a lift to Ballyfermot in the army truck was, however, the highlight of my Communion day, and I was more pleased that CIE was on strike than all the money I collected. The photograph shows me grinning toothless at the camera in my white dress and shiny shoes.

I cried for Ireland when my brother Davy set off for London. I thought I would never see him again. Then one day a guard knocked at the door to tell my mother he was being deported from the island of Guernsey because he had no work and was sleeping on the beaches. It was the one and only time I was happy to see a guard at the door.

Though my father eventually found work doing security for a building contractor, he still hadn't stopped drinking. When my sister Sandra was getting married, he fell in the night before the wedding, legless and threw £50 at her feet.

'There's your fucking wedding present. You can walk up the aisle by yourself, because I won't be there,' he said.

He tried to burn his new wedding suit in the fire that night, but he must have had a change of heart because he turned up on her proud day, the worse for wear as usual.

Sandra was 25 when she got married. After she moved to her own place, she and her husband, Joe, often took me on daytrips as a treat. My favourite was the mystery trip when she'd pack up the flask and sandwiches and we'd all head down to Connolly Station and board the train. Only the train driver knew where we were going; you see it was a mystery train. More often than not it was to Boyle in Co. Roscommon. A wonderful place when the sun was shining.

I was eleven when the last of my brothers got married. My father had been sacked from his security job and he was back to his usual tricks again. Labour day came, he washed and shaved himself early, and left to sign on down at the dole office. If we were lucky we'd see him again when he fell in that night after closing time. Sometimes two days could go by without sight of him. When he did appear he was penniless, leaving my mother to borrow. She was a quiet, gentle, respectable woman and very independent. I'll always remember her sitting in the armchair opposite the kitchen window, waiting for my father's shadow to pass. There was many a time on labour day that I searched the pubs in Thomas St. with her, hoping this one was not going to be like the last. More often than not it was. The rest of the week he'd sit in his chair, depressed because he had no money. He was a pitiful sight. When I'd come home from school, my mother would usher me upstairs to the bedroom, where she'd have the kettle ready for tea and a sandwich. There was no food for my father, 'It's his doing,' she'd say.

Life went on like this, day after day. Despite my father's objection to education, I continued to love school and do well at it. My brothers and sister had left at 14 to go out to work. But that wasn't going to be me. I was going on to do my Leaving Cert. First, however, I had to get through my Inter Cert. I knew I was smart and that if I worked hard I could get a good job when I finished school.

Our English teacher, Mrs. Dolan, was tall with dark, shoulder length hair and glasses. She was always very well dressed and she spoke ever so grand. I always liked English. I developed a passion for reading when I was very small, and joined the library. This love began with a book called *Mrs Pepperpot* by Alf Proysen, a Norwegian writer. It was a lovely story of the adventures of an old woman who shrinks at the strangest of times and gets up to all kinds of mischief. I think I must have read every one in the series.

As part of our education, Mrs. Dolan decided to bring the class to see a play at the Abbey Theatre. I was thrilled as I'd never been to a play before. It was *Juno and the Paycock* by Sean O'Casey and I loved all the Dublin characters especially Mrs. Boyle. She reminded me of my own mam. I sat with my friends, Una and Maria and we laughed at Joxer's antics and cried with Mrs. Tancred when 'her darlin' son was riddled with bullets'. But I became distracted by the boys' class, seated in the row in front of us. One of them kept looking back at me. That was how I met Tony. He waited for me afterwards and asked me if I'd go out with him. He was my first love.

He lived on the northside of Dublin, which made it quite difficult for us to see each other very often. I'd lie awake at night, wondering when our next date would be, picturing his pale blue eyes, his smile. I remember him bringing me back to meet his mother. I was so nervous. His house seemed so big compared to our little flat. It overlooked the sea and we spent evenings walking hand in hand along the pier, listening to the waves lapping against its side. I was so happy then, but it didn't last long. We both knew our exams were coming up soon so we agreed to go our separate ways, having made a solemn promise always to keep in touch.

My Inter Cert was over, I was fifteen. I had managed to do well, with four honours and three passes. I failed one subject, German, because my German teacher and I never got on from the word go. His name was Mr. Anderson, a giant of a man. One day he pleaded with me.

'Please Anna, why don't you leave school and get a factory job?'

But I was having none of it.

'I'm going to do my Leaving Cert and get a good job,' I said, brazenly back to him.

Since childhood my mother had always been very protective of me, as I was the youngest and the smallest, her baby. I wasn't allowed to mix with the other children in the flats. It wasn't until my teenage years that I became friendly with a girl who lived in the next block. Her name was Jacinta. We liked the same music, the music of the 1960s. We became modettes. Every Saturday we would search the vintage shops for clothes or shoes that we could wear. I'd pick out a tweed skirt or jacket, Jacinta might go for a polo neck jumper and ski pants, or I'd kit myself out in a green parka jacket with a target on the back, black pants and winkle-picker shoes, and the two of us would sashay down O'Connell St., my hair cut in a bob style.

There was also another girl I became friendly with who lived in Jacinta's block, and her name was Linda. She, like myself, wasn't allowed to mix much, though I did go to a dance with her and her sister one night. My first disco. It was held in All Hallows' College in Drumcondra. That's where I met Paul. He was sitting beside the D.J. box dressed in his mod clothes, looking totally lost. He spotted me and asked me to dance. We danced the night away and later made a date.

My mother liked Paul. 'He's a nice lad,' she said, after hearing his father worked with my cousin. He was working too, doing his apprenticeship in spray painting. Paul was eighteen, had a great sense of humour and always made me laugh. That was one of the things I liked about him. I could talk to him about anything, he was more like a brother to me.

I got a part-time job that summer as a lounge girl in a local pub. It was cheap labour, but the money helped towards my books. I was happy enough to be still seeing Paul, although he was starting to get serious about me and wanted to see me every night. His mother got fed up with him never staying in any more, so much so that she locked him in his room one night. That still didn't stop him. He got out the window, climbed down the drainpipe and made his way towards me.

But I attracted someone else's eye that summer. I didn't know who he was, but I thought he must live locally, since everytime I set foot outside the door he was there, winking at me. One night on my way home from work he introduced himself. His name was Simon.

'I live over the road. Do you fancy coming out with me tomorrow night?'

I said no, as I was still with Paul.

He kept pestering me until I gave in.

'OK then, Wednesday. Under Clery's clock at eight. We can go to the pictures if you'd like?'

God, what have I done? I thought to myself. How am I going to explain this to Paul? I didn't want to go behind his back, so the following day I told him.

Paul took the news bad. I could see the hurt in his eyes. I knew how much he really loved me, but going out with

Simon seemed exciting. He was everything a girl could ask for, tall with fair hair and blue eyes.

Wednesday night came and I got a bus into town. I was late but Simon was there waiting. We went to see *Octopussy*, a James Bond movie. When he turned to kiss me, our teeth banged off one another which made us both giggle. On our way home we stopped at McDonalds for Coke. As we walked through town, a homeless boy handed him a piece of paper. It was a begging letter. Simon delved into his pocket and gave him some money. I was touched by his kind-heartedness.

As he walked me up the steps to our flat, he turned to kiss me goodnight. It was then I saw Paul standing there. He was holding something in his jacket, and I could see he was full of rage. I quickly said goodnight to Simon, urging him to leave. Paul took a knife from his pocket and burst into tears. He just stood there, holding the weapon, not knowing what to do with it. I told him I couldn't go on seeing him. I was still only sixteen, after all. He put the knife back in his pocket and disappeared into the dark. But that didn't deter Paul and he came down the next night and many nights after that. He wanted us to get engaged and told me of his plans to buy the ring that Christmas. He began sending me love letters, poems and songs in the post, but I refused to see him. I couldn't bear the thought of him coming over anymore. I thought that would be the end of it.

One night as I was going for a walk with Simon, I noticed Paul following us.

'I want to talk to you,' he said to Simon.

So off they went, the two of them and left me standing there. After about five minutes, they came back and said to me, 'Anna, which one of us do you want to go out with?'

I was speechless, but knew I had to make up my mind.

After some time I turned to Paul and said, 'I'm sorry, Paul, but I've already made my decision.'

He turned and walked away and I knew I had really hurt him when he had done nothing to deserve it.

But he still didn't give up. The letters, poems and songs continued. He now wanted me to go to his Debs Ball and had already bought the tickets. He said if I wasn't going to accompany him, then he wouldn't go at all. After much consideration, I agreed to his request.

CHAPTER 2

Simon lived across the road in an older block of flats. He had been adopted as a young baby by his grandparents. Their daughter Celia was his real mother. He didn't discover this until he was twelve years old. He always referred to Celia as his sister and his grandparents would always be his mam and dad. This being established, Simon's family was indeed a large one. There was Rita, Bernie, Angela, Mags, Tricia, Jane, Celia, Max, Pat, Liam, Bill, and Noel. Twelve in all. These he called his brothers and sisters, even though they were his aunts and uncles; each of whom by now had married and left home.

Only Simon remained.

I got on really well with his mam and dad, Elsie and Paddy. Now getting on in years, they were an old-fashioned couple who were much respected and set in their ways. They had raised a good family. Two of their sons, Max and Pat, had their own plumbing business. Simon worked for Max. The first time he brought me home to meet them, Elsie had tea cakes made for me. She gave me a big hug at the door and welcomed me.

I was now in my fifth year at secondary school. I picked my subjects carefully for my Leaving Cert. As you can imagine I dropped German. I was doing honours English and Maths, with the rest at pass level. Studying became hard with Simon around. We wanted to see each other every night. We usually just went for a walk and talked about our hopes and dreams, music and clothes. He wasn't into the mod scene and saw himself more as a new romantic. He listened to bands like the Human League, Duran Duran and ABC who were popular at the time. This was real love.

Simon knew I was going to Paul's Debs soon. He kept telling me how much he loved me, and didn't want me to go. He was scared that Paul and I would get back together again. He said if I really loved him, I'd let him make love to me. In that way he'd know how much he meant to me. Then it just happened one night when Elsie and Paddy went off on their weekly visits and Simon invited me up to the flat to listen to his new Human League LP.

The night of the Debs, Paul arrived carrying his orchid and a box of chocolates. I had rented a lilac satin dress, and wished it was Simon and not Paul who was telling me I looked gorgeous. We had dinner in Jury's, and dancing later at the Olympic Ballroom. All night long, he pleaded with me to go back out with him. My mind was deep in thought. I knew he had to understand that we had no future. When he walked me home I said goodbye and told him I never wanted to see him again. I watched his face crumble, but there must have been something in my voice that made him finally accept my words that it was over between us. He never contacted me after that.

I called over to Simon's next day. He wasn't at home but Elsie was. She brought me in.

'Did you have a good night last night, lass?'

'I did, Elsie.'

'Simon was worried about you. He sat at the window all night long waiting for you to come home.'

We both laughed, but then her face grew serious.

'Sit down, Anna, I want to tell you something. Simon hasn't been going to work at all lately and I'm getting worried about him. He's starting to hang around with a bad lot. There's been some right gurriers calling for him these last couple of days. Just take my advice; don't let yourself down to him. You're only young yet.'

I understood her words, but it was too late for them now, I was in love with Simon. Still her words worried me. There was so much I didn't know about this fella I was in love with. Where was he going the last couple of days? Whose company was he keeping? There were so many questions I needed to ask, but still there was no sign of him coming home. I waited as long as I could for him to return, but I waited in vain.

'Elsie, when he comes in, tell him I've called, and I want to talk to him.'

'OK, love, but if I was you I'd give him up,' she said as I headed towards the door. I looked at her. They were very strong words from a woman who loved him so much.

'Maybe I will, Elsie, maybe I will.'

I was only in my own door, when my mother collared me.

'I want to talk to you.'

'What is it, Mam?'

'I've been hearing nothing but bad stories about that Simon you're hanging around with.'

'What kind of stories?'

'Some poor woman's handbag was taken today down the street. All the neighbours were out with the screams of her. One of them said it was Simon that did it. I don't want you having anymore to do with him. Do you hear me? He's no use, Anna.'

I was shocked and devastated. I couldn't believe it. I wouldn't believe it. It wasn't him. Why would he do such a horrible thing? After all he had a nice family, a good job … and me. The neighbour was wrong. She had to be.

It was nine o'clock that night when I heard someone whistling at the back of the flats. It was Simon. I was very angry at the thoughts of him stealing anything, never mind a woman's bag. I crept down the stairs and out the hall door.

'Where were you all day? I went over to Elsie's looking for you and waited half the day, with no sign of you?'

'I was working; we had a job on in Cabinteely. Why?' he asked.

'I don't believe you, that's why. A woman's handbag was stolen today in the flats and a neighbour told my mother it was you that did it.'

'And you believe her? I was working in Cabinteely plumbing out a new house; ask Max if you like. He's only after dropping me down. You don't believe me, do you?'

'I want to believe you. How do you explain those gurriers calling for you then?'

'What gurriers, Anna? I don't know what you're talking about.'

'Elsie said some fellas knocked for you today.'

'I don't know anything about that. Sure I wasn't there, was I?'

He had an answer for everything.

Christmas was coming. Elsie and Paddy were spending the holidays out at Tricia's house. Simon was going too.

'I don't want to go without you, but Elsie and Paddy said I have to. They don't want me in the flat on my own for Christmas. Tricia's having a party. Ask your mother can you come?'

'I think I already know the answer to that one. There's no way I'll be allowed go to Skerries with you.'

'I'll miss you so much, Anna. Look, I've bought you some things for Christmas.'

'Where did you get the money?'

'I'm working, amn't I?'

He had bought me a jumper, a skirt and a pair of suede boots. My suspicions were aroused again and then quickly dismissed when he sent me a gigantic Christmas card vowing to love me for all eternity. In return I surprised him with Diana Ross's Motown hits LP.

I called over to see Elsie too, and gave her the slippers I had bought. She was really pleased since her old ones had seen their day. She hugged me, slipping something into my hand.

'And this is for you.'

It was a small box and inside was a gold chain with my initials on it. As she fastened the clip around my neck she whispered in my ear, 'Anna, despite all I've said about him, you're the lass for Simon. Look after him when I'm gone.'

I nodded. Sadly the thoughts of Elsie going anywhere upset me. She and Paddy had grown close to me and I had really grown close to them. They seemed such an odd match. He was a fine big man. When he spoke, the words bellowed from his mouth. She was a tiny woman, softly spoken and always with such wit. Like chalk and cheese.

Christmas Eve came and Simon was very upset leaving, unnecessarily so, because he arrived at my door on Christmas night having walked most of his way from Skerries. I was delighted to see him, and even more delighted when my mother asked him in.

CHAPTER 3

The Leaving Cert was six months away and I was starting to panic. I had to knuckle down and study or time would slip away on me. I had my plans made. I was going to do well and achieve the points I needed to study Sociology in UCD. I was going to be a social worker.

Simon would have to be told we couldn't see each other as often as we had been. But I was also worried about what he was doing with his free time? Why did he spend so long in the bathroom at Elsie's? Was he sick or something? Elsie and Paddy had their own suspicions, especially when Paddy found a bottle of vinegar in the toilet. Something was going on.

Then my periods were late and a different kind of panic set it. I was sick with worry, but Simon was no help at all. He didn't seem to care when I told him that I was late. He seemed to be on another planet altogether. Each time I met him I was noticing big changes in his behaviour. And there were the lies.

I was at my wits' end. I didn't know who to turn to. I certainly couldn't tell my mother considering the opinion she had of Simon, nor could I tell my sister even though she just had her own baby. I had to tell someone so I confided in Celia. She sprang into action and brought me to the local maternity hospital for a pregnancy test. As I handed in my sample of urine, I prayed that the result would be negative.

The nurse returned shortly with a big smile on her face.

'Your test is positive. You're pregnant.'

Not a word passed my lips. I was speechless. Then I broke down and cried. After I had pulled myself together a bit, I told Celia that I wanted to see Simon, so she brought me to Elsie's. Elsie was out, but Simon was in his room. I went up to it and stood in the doorway.

'Simon, I'm pregnant.'

'What?'

'I'm pregnant.'

'You're not, are you? Listen, I have to go out for a while. I'll be back after. See ya.'

And he was gone.

No words of love, compassion, understanding or support. Nothing. Just out the door as if he had nothing to do with me, as if he wasn't the father of the child I carried inside me. Here was the man I had given my body and love to, who had changed so much that I was finding it hard to recognise him.

It was my brother, Davy, who told my mother that I was pregnant; I didn't have the heart. I knew this would shatter all the dreams she had for me. She was hysterical.

'You don't know what you've let yourself in for, Anna. How could you have let yourself down to him? That yoke. What about your schooling?'

'I'm going to speak to Sr. Mary tomorrow, Mam. I'm sorry I let you down. But don't worry. Simon'll look after me.'

She laughed.

'He's not doing a good job of that now, is he? I told you a long time ago he was no use.'

I started to cry.

'It's many a salt tear you'll cry yet. You'll regret the day you ever laid eyes on him.'

How could she see what I wouldn't?

Davy told my father too. I wasn't around that day to hear his words or see the expression in his face, but I could easily imagine it.

After the initial shock, Simon came to grips with the idea of me being pregnant. He told Elsie, Paddy and the rest of his family. Elsie and Paddy being old-fashioned and honourable, told him to do the right thing. And so the pressure started for us to be married as soon as possible. There was one major problem. I was still only sixteen and it hadn't been in my plans.

I gathered up my courage and spoke to Sr. Mary, the principal of my secondary school. I was very nervous. When I told her, she wasn't as shocked as I had expected her to be, but instead was kind and sympathetic. She could see how anxious I was still to do my Leaving Cert. She knew I was determined not to throw my education away because I was pregnant. Sr. Mary offered to help all she could. I was delighted when she agreed to allow me to stay in school as long as I wanted, and if I wished I could sit my exam in a school in Navan. In that way I would avoid any snide comments and nobody need know of my predicament. I was going to do that exam one way or the other.

It was a bitter cold March day, when Simon and I went into town to do some shopping. After buying some fruit in Moore St., we continued on into Dunnes Stores to get the groceries for my mother. I was standing in the queue and almost at the checkout desk when Simon got down on bended knee and produced a box from his pocket. The customers stared in awe as I stood red-faced. Simon opened the tiny box.

'Will you marry me, Anna?'

Totally stunned, he slipped the engagement ring onto my finger. It had five diamond stones mounted on an 18ct gold band.

'I will.'

I studied the diamonds, the gold band.

'It's beautiful, but where did you get the money?'

'Max owed it to me, and I've been saving up for it for a while now.'

My mother on the other hand had a different reaction.

'So you think you're getting married do you? Over my dead body.'

'Not just yet, Mam. I'm going to do my exams, have the baby and then …'

'You're only sixteen for God's sake. You have the whole of your life in front of you. Stop seeing life through rose-tinted glasses, Anna.'

Why could she not just be happy for me?

When I went to school the following day, Una couldn't believe the news. 'You're pregnant and engaged to be married? What about your exams?'

'I'm not getting married yet. I'm going to do my Leaving Cert first.'

I swore her to secrecy about my pregnancy. However news of my engagement travelled fast. English class began with Mrs Dolan asking, 'Anna Mahon, is it true what I've been hearing?'

'Yes, Miss.'

'When's the big day?'

'We haven't set a date yet. I'm doing my exams first.'

'Right you are too. Put your love life on the back burner until these are over. Now back to work everyone,' she roared.

I hid my face in my poetry book, pretending to read the Lake Isle of Inisfree and seeing no words. Little did she know the position I had found myself in.

Simon came to me one day in a terrible state.

'Elsie and Paddy have told me to pack my bags and get out. They're sick of me. I'm going over to stay in Celia's.'

I looked at him. I was puzzled. I knew how much Elsie and Paddy loved him. I also knew that something really serious must have happened for them to take such action.

'I don't believe they did this just because they're sick of you?'

'What do you mean?'

'Did you have a row with them or something?'

'No, why?'

'I'm only asking.'

'Look, you know things haven't been so great since I got you pregnant. We just haven't been getting on well lately.'

'If you want to move over to Celia's, that's fine, but I don't think she'll have you.'

'Ah. She will. I'll give her some money each week. That'll keep her happy. Listen when are we getting married anyway? I'm sick of not seeing you as often now because of all this studying you're doing.'

I told him I wanted to do my exams before I did anything else.

'We'll get married after I have the baby.'

'So you're putting your exams before me now, are you? The sooner we're married and have our own place, the better. That's the way I see it. I'm going to ask you once more, give up school and marry me.'

'Well if you're going to be so unreasonable about it, maybe it would be better if we stopped seeing each other until my exams are over.'

'Look I don't need this. Fuck you. Give me my ring back. You can keep your schooling.'

I pulled the ring off my finger and handed it back to him. No one was going to tell me what to do. With that he stormed off. He had become so unreasonable that I didn't know what to make of him. I realised again how much he had changed. Were Elsie and Paddy putting so much pressure on him to do the honourable thing and get married that he could no longer stand the strain? We could work this one out, but first I'd have to talk to Elsie.

When I called over to her the following day, she was seated in her usual position, on her hardbacked chair in the kitchen. She looked sad.

'Hi Elsie. What is it?'

'I heard you two fell out last night and you gave him back the ring. Well, you did the right thing, lass. You shouldn't have let yourself down to him. I told you, but you wouldn't listen.'

She lifted the tea-towel that lay in her lap and wiped her eyes.

'I love him, Elsie. We had a row yesterday, that's all.'

'Sit here beside me, lass,' and she moved some clothes from the chair next to her. I sat down.

'I don't know how I'm going to tell you this.'

My stomach churned.

'Simon hasn't been himself lately since he stopped working with Max. He's hanging around with a bad lot. That doorbell never stops ringing. Yesterday Paddy wanted to use the toilet, but Simon was in the bathroom and he couldn't get in. He must have been a good quarter of an hour waiting on him to come out. So he pushed in the door to see what was keeping him. There he was standing up against the wall with a string around his arm and a needle sticking in him. He's on the needle, Anna. Paddy had murder with him. He told him to get his stuff and go; he was never to call here again. You did the right thing not having any more to do with him, lass.'

'He's on the needle?'

The words swirled round in my head. Simon was on drugs. Everything now slotted into place, his lies, his mood swings, his lack of motivation and absenteeism from work. I thought back to when Paddy found a bottle of vinegar in the toilet. How long had this been going on? A good while I reckoned. I felt betrayed. I sat there and looked at Elsie's sad face. I put my arms around her and told her she was doing the right thing too.

'You're welcome up here anytime, lass. The door is always open.'

I left totally bewildered. How could he do this to me? Did he love me at all or had he only used me? And what was I going to do now? I was sixteen, three months pregnant and the man I loved and hoped to marry had just turned out to be a junkie.

For the next couple of days I walked around in a stupor. I kept asking myself the same questions over and over again. I couldn't concentrate in school, even to open a book seemed a major effort and so my studies suffered. As the days passed I heard nothing from him.

Then about a week later, I was reading in my room when I heard that same whistle I had grown so accustomed to. His whistles echoed throughout the flats. I dropped the book and made for the front door. He was halfway up the landing when I met him.

'What do you mean echoing the place like that?'

'I had to talk to you.'

'Well I don't want to talk to you. You're nothing but a liar, a cheat, a robber and a drug addict. How could I have been so naïve? Just clear off and leave me alone. I never want to see you again.'

'Please, I can explain.' He grabbed my arms roughly. 'Come on, we're going on a walk away from here. We need to have a serious talk. You've got to let me explain myself.'

Reluctantly I walked keeping my distance from him. Nothing he said was going to change my mind.

'Anna, you know I love you. I'm sorry for being so unreasonable about your exams. I know how much they mean to you. I'm not a liar, robber or a junkie. I never touched drugs in my life.'

'Who d'you think you're fooling? I didn't come up the Liffey on a bike. You were caught over in Elsie's with a needle sticking out of your arm. You're a fucking liar.'

I saw his expression change.

'Who told you about that? It was my ma. Wasn't it?'

'It doesn't matter who told me. I know it's true.'

'Right, let me tell you. I was over at the sheds one night having a few drinks with the lads when this fella offered it to me.'

'Offered what?'

'A turn-on, gear, smack, heroin … whatever you want to call it. Anyway he put the gear into a works and skin-popped it for me.'

'That bottle of vinegar that Paddy found in the toilet had something to do with this, hadn't it?'

'Yeh. I used the vinegar because it has acetic acid in it to break down the gear. You can use lemons as well.'

'Oh, can you now? Wouldn't I have been much better if I knew that the last time I had a lemon? Well, I'm telling you now, I don't give a shit about your lemons, your vinegar or your drugs. I just want to figure out how long this has been going on. You've been on drugs even before I met you, haven't you?'

'No, I haven't. I told you all this happened only a few weeks ago. I'm not addicted, Anna. I can give it up if I want to. I promise.'

'It's too late now for promises. You've sickened me with all your lies and stories. I don't want to see you anymore. It's over.'

The words were barely out of my mouth when he lunged forward and punched me in the stomach. I coiled up in pain, writhing.

'My baby, my baby, you bastard.'

He was pulling me to my feet, his arms around me, tears rolling down his face.

'I'm sorry, Anna. I'm sorry, I'm sorry. I didn't mean to do it. Honest I didn't. You wouldn't listen to me. Please don't say it's over. I don't want to lose you. You mean too much to me.'

His words were as empty as my father's pockets, but I didn't argue for fear he might strike again. I waited until I was in the safety of the flats before I said, 'I can't take this any more. It's over, now get away from me.'

He turned away and his face was soaked with tears.

'I'm sorry Anna,' he said, and then he was gone.

I didn't tell my mother what really happened. I just said we had a big argument and that I never wanted to lay eyes on him again. My mother was relieved. The pain in my stomach subsided, but I couldn't help worrying something might be wrong with the baby.

CHAPTER 4

I continued going to school though I now found it even harder to concentrate on my studies, but I was still determined to plough ahead. I dropped my higher-level subjects as I decided it was better to get good passes than failed honours. My sister Sandra had made an appointment at the maternity hospital for me and the date was fast approaching. Until then it was head in the books.

Sandra came with me to the hospital. I was glad to have her with me as I didn't know what to expect. The doctor checked my blood pressure and my weight and told me I was doing fine. I told him about the pain I had. I was very anxious about what he might find. He produced a cone-shaped object and pressed it to my stomach. He smiled and said everything was fine; that the pain was due to my baby lying on a nerve.

'From my dates, he says I'm due at the end of August,' I told Sandra who was waiting outside to hear the news. She was all excited, but I couldn't share her enthusiasm. At that moment, both my body and mind were in a state of fatigue and worry. I went home to rest.

The days and nights passed. The pain was still so severe I wasn't able to go to school. The whistling continued. Whenever a caller came, my mother answered the door. It wasn't long until Simon was one of those callers.

'Hello, Mrs. Mahon. Can I see Anna for a minute?'

'She doesn't want to see you.'

'I need to see her, to talk to her.'

'I told you already she doesn't want to see you. Is it you that's whistling the flats down each night?'

'I'm sorry, Mrs. Mahon.'

'Don't knock on this door again, do you hear me? Now off with you.'

I lay on the sofa exhausted.

'I don't think he's ever going to leave me alone, Mam.'

I turned into the sofa, the tears filling my eyes. I don't know how long I was asleep, when I was woken by a commotion at the hall door. I lay there motionless, listening to the angry voices at my doorstep. Simon was back again and this time he wasn't alone. He had brought his birth mother, Celia, over to plead his case.

'My son, Simon, tells me, Mrs. Mahon that you're stopping him from seeing his Anna. Is that true?'

'Listen here to me. You don't come up knocking at my door with that attitude. It's up to Anna herself if she wants to see Simon and right now she doesn't. So go and leave the girl in peace.'

'But, Mrs. Mahon, he has to see her, to talk to her about the future of his child. Wouldn't it be grand if they got a little place of their own? It wouldn't matter if they had to sit on orange boxes once they had each other, isn't that right, Mrs. Mahon?'

'She doesn't want to see him, let alone live with him.'

'Let her tell him herself then. Where is she?'

With that Celia barged past my mother calling me, Simon in close pursuit.

'Anna, how are you, love? There's someone here to see you.'

I didn't respond. I lay there wishing the world would end as her voice got nearer and nearer. 'Do you still want to go out with Simon, Anna?'

Over and over she repeated the question until finally she was only inches away. There she stood glaring at me. She prodded me with her finger. Infuriated I yelled, 'Fuck off out of my home. You've no right coming into it in the first place. You're not welcome here. There's the door,' and pointing to Simon I continued, 'and on your way out bring him with you, I never want to see him again.'

Celia was so shocked at my sudden outburst, she quickly turned on her heel, Simon following after her.

As soon as the pain ceased, I began to prepare myself for my return to school. I was very anxious to achieve my main goal in life. The day before I returned my classmate Una came to tell me that the news of my pregnancy was all over the school. Another sixth year student Denise was busy telling all and sundry about how she had seen me in a maternity dress.

But these stories failed to turn me into just another 'drop-out.' Part of me was now even more determined to sit my exams and pass them, yet the thoughts of both students and teachers looking down their noses at me made me even more upset. As it happened, I couldn't have been more wrong. I walked into my class to cheers and applause. It was going to work out after all. I got back into work with renewed hope.

Simon continued to whistle and call to the house, but without welcome.

One of these occasions still remains fresh in my mind. It was a sunny Saturday afternoon and Sandra was in the kitchen with me doing some ironing, when there was a knock at the door. I went to see who it was and he was just standing there. Unlike other previous occasions he was clean-shaven, well groomed and with new attire. My attitude towards him was still unchanged.

'Anna, please. I wanted to see you. I've changed, honest I have. I don't use drugs anymore. I'm clean. I've been attending Jervis St. They had me on a Physeptone course, daily doses of the stuff to wean me off the gear. Now, I've done it.'

'Well, congratulations,' I said, not believing a word.

He didn't read the sarcasm in my voice.

'Yeh, I've done it, Anna. I'm even back working with Max. Look, I came up to give you this; it's a few bob for you and the baby.'

In his outstretched hand was a roll of money.

'I don't want your rotten money. I don't want anything off you ever again. Do you not understand what I'm saying or something?'

'Anna, please take it. You'll need it for the baby. I am the father after all. I miss you so much. Why are you doing this to me? You know how much I love you, need you, and want you back.' He was on his knees again, except this time for a different reason.

'Please, Anna, please say you'll give me a second chance.'

'It's over. It's over. I don't want you or your fucking money. Now leave me alone.'

With that he caught my arms and started to drag me down, tears running down his face and froth pouring from his mouth.

'Leave me alone, leave me alone,' I screamed. He stood up and straightened himself.

'So me and my money is no good. Is that it?' He unrolled the wad of notes that he held in his hand. 'You don't want the fucking money so. Well I don't want it either.'

As I closed the door, I watched him rip the notes into shreds, the fragments falling to the ground and scattering all around his feet. I just left them there and went back into the room. Sandra was all ears, waiting to hear the news.

'Well, what was all that about?'

'Just the usual, you know, off the drugs, back working, all that rubbish, begging me to go back with him. Had a load of money, wanted me to take it for the baby.'

'And did you?'

'I did not. I told him I didn't want him or his rotten money.'

'So what did he do?'

'He ripped it all up to pieces.'

'And the bits? Where are they?'

'I don't know; I closed the door on him.'

Hearing that she jumped up off the chair and headed out into the hall.

'Where are you going? What are you doing?'

'To see if they're still there, silly.'

She opened the door; every fragment of the shredded notes was gone.

'I was going to stick the bits back together again, Anna, but obviously someone beat me to it. He's not as thick as I thought he was.'

With that we both fell around laughing. It was the first laugh I'd had in a long time.

The day of my exams finally arrived. I was six months pregnant and feeling every ounce of it. I desperately wanted to do well, and so I had put myself under enormous pressure by trying to cram all my studying before each exam. I got through as best I could, and tried to reassure myself that even if I failed, I had done my best, though I worried a lot about it as I waited for the results. I felt I could have done a lot better under different circumstances. I prayed to God that my results wouldn't let me down, but for now all I could do was wait in hope that I had passed.

It was one night during that summer as I was getting ready for bed that I heard this loud bang at the back of the flats. Voices echoed in the night's stillness. The following day I learned that a safe had been stolen and was thrown from the roof of a local building.

But I couldn't worry about that now. I had a lot of other things on my mind. How bad were the pains of labour? Would my baby be all right? And how was I going to cope being a single mother? These and many other thoughts filled my mind. I was scared. I tried to talk to Sandra about it, but she changed the subject. That made me even more worried.

The days and nights that followed seemed like an eternity to me. On returning from yet another hospital visit, I opened the hall door to find the flat in total disarray. My mother and my brother Davy stood looking bewildered and confused.

'What's wrong, Mam? What happened?'

'Davy, tell her.'

'There was a knock at the door while Ma was down doing the shopping. Three guards stood there with a search warrant, looking for a red-haired woman and a young man. I told them there was no one here with red hair and that I didn't live here myself but I let them in to search. Apparently the jeweller's up the road was robbed, and they were looking for the stolen jewellery.'

'They have the place upside down. They even looked in the fridge. I can't believe this has happened. Why? That's what I'd like to know.'

My mother was in a state.

Davy offered to make her some tea to settle her nerves. I followed him into the kitchen.

'Did the guards say anything else?'

'Yeh, They did. When they were searching the bedrooms upstairs, they found a photo of you in the jewellery box. They asked me who you were and where you were? I said you were my sister and you were out on an ante-natal visit at the hospital.'

'What? They were asking about me?'

Why would they be asking about me? Who would have given our address to the guards? None of us was ever in any trouble with the law and that was one thing my mother could always be proud of. Now here she was devastated by the shame of three guards calling at her door and turning the few possessions she had upside down and inside out. The guards told us that someone had given our address as a tip off. The whole incident of our home being searched aroused a lot of suspicion that left us with many unanswered questions. We never got to the bottom of what happened that day.

CHAPTER 5

It was August 15th 1984, exam results day. I was both nervous and excited at the same time. I knew my results would be sent to the school, and because of my condition I asked my mother to collect them for me. She said she would. It was a short journey from the flats to the convent. I sat by the bedroom window awaiting her return. As the minutes ticked slowly by, I wondered how it could take her so long to come home. It could only mean one thing; she was too upset to face me. After what seemed a lifetime, I spotted her reassuring figure in the distance. When she reached the corner of the flats she waved the envelope ecstatically. Trying desperately not to raise too much hope, I ran down the stairs to the door. I met her hurrying up the landing, out of breath as she handed me the brown envelope. Franticly, I opened it. Three honours and three passes. I flung my arms around my mother.

'I got it Mam, I got it.'

'I met Sr. Mary at the school door. If ever there was someone happy you had passed, it was her. She said you deserved it. She said there was a fair few failed; not all the faces were happy ones.'

I was touched at how kind and supportive Sr. Mary had been through all of this. I don't know how I would have made it without her kindness. Delighted, I stuck my Leaving Cert results to the wall for all the family to see. When they came in, there were congratulations all round.

It was three more weeks before the baby was due. I started arranging some baby clothes and night dresses for the hospital. I occupied my time knitting little cardigans. In my dreaming moments I wondered if I might be able to make it to my debs dance on the nineteenth of September. But first I had to have my baby. I tried to ask Sandra again about giving birth. Seeing that she was a mother herself, I thought she would help me prepare for this big moment, but all I could get out of her was that when the apple was ripe it would fall.

The days turned to weeks.

On my next appointment at the hospital, the doctors said the date of delivery was wrong. They expected the birth to occur now in late September. I was so disappointed and impatient. Time passed even more slowly. September 19th came and went. I watched out my bedroom window as my schoolmates, in their classy debs dresses, exotic orchids pinned on the shoulder, and sophisticated hairstyles, stepped into taxis with their beaus. The rippling of laughter filled the night air.

'Mam, quick, get up. I've started.'

It was about 6am, Thursday morning the 11th of October. I was in the height of pain as I called out to her. Like lightening she was up and dressed, and we set out into the cold chilly morning. The street was empty except for the odd straggler here and there. She thought it would be quicker if we started walking our way up to the hospital, which was as well, as on our way a large warehouse was on fire. Flames shot into the sky and smoke billowed around us. The guards and fire brigades were at the scene. Traffic was at a standstill. There was commotion everywhere. The pain was so intense I crawled up against a wall and closed my eyes. I didn't care what happened to me. I just wanted to die. Next thing I knew I was in a car, passing out, with my mother slapping my face to keep me awake. The driver (and to this day I don't know who he was) drove us at great speed until we were at the maternity hospital.

They did their routine check and pronounced me to be in labour. Funny but I could have told them that myself for nothing. I was put into the labour ward and the pain was so bad I was given gas. Even with that, I was screaming with pain when the Sister came over and said, 'you're not the only woman in this ward that's having a baby. So for goodness sake, stay quiet.' Some bedside manner she had.

The nurse came by to check my progress and suddenly I was being rushed into the delivery room.

'Push, Anna, Push.'

'Pant now.'

'Another push.'

'And another.'

'It's a boy.'

The cord was cut and my baby was handed to me, my very own baby. I was flooded with emotion as I kissed his tiny nose. He looked so much like Simon it was heartbreaking.

'He's a right bouncer, isn't he, Mam? Two ounces short of ten pound.'

I couldn't believe I was finally holding my beautiful boy.

Some hours later, I awoke to the sound of a baby crying by my bedside. It took me a few minutes to realise that he was mine and that this was my responsibility now. He was hungry and was due his feed. I didn't have any difficulty feeding him, unlike the other mothers. On the contrary, he was such a hungry baby there was just no filling him. But he was mine and I wouldn't have swapped him for all the tea in China. I called him Damien. Sandra laughed when I told her, 'You're calling him Damien, I hope he isn't anything like the other Damien out of that film *The Omen*.'

'No, Sandra, this one's an angel,' I said and we both had a giggle. The little cardigans I had spent the entire summer knitting proved to be very little indeed. He was so big not one of them fitted him. Instead I gave them to Sandra's daughter Linda to put on her dolls. That was all they were fit for.

I had lots of visitors during my stay at the hospital. It seemed everyone wanted to see the new arrival. My family, friends and well wishers all flocked to my bedside, but somehow I found myself watching the proud fathers calling with their gifts and flowers to see their spouses and newborn babies. I wished things could have been different and that Simon was one of them. I just longed to return home.

CHAPTER 6

It wasn't long before I realised just how difficult life was going to be as a single parent. Back home Damien cried constantly for his feeds, and satisfying his hunger occupied most of my days and nights. My mother and Sandra helped me out whenever they could and gave me the break I sometimes badly needed. I had the basic necessities; but these didn't include a pram or a cot. Damien slept in a carrycot belonging to my nephew David. When I did need to travel anywhere I carried him in his baby nest. Some bunch of roses this life.

He was almost two weeks old when my mother and I brought him into town. I was in the ILAC Centre when I noticed someone following us. Damien was in his baby nest. Simon walked past several times peering in at the bundle I cradled in my arms. I held my baby close to me, protecting him. I knew how much Simon wanted to see him, but I was in no humour to show him any compassion. It didn't take him long to get the message and he disappeared into the shopping crowds. That was my baby's first introduction to his father.

Damien was six weeks old when he took sick. I was going out with Lisa that night and knew something was wrong when he wouldn't settle. His eyes rolled in his little head and his cries turned into high-pitched piercing screams. When my mother became alarmed I knew it had to be serious. She took him in her arms. 'Come on quick. We have to get him to the hospital.'

The children's hospital was nearby so we didn't have far to run. I was by now hysterical. When we rushed into casualty, there was no waiting around to be seen; the nurse whipped Damien straight from my mother's arms and was gone. The nurse at the desk asked for the particulars. Shaking I gave his name, age and address.

The doctor came out and called my mother and me into a room and sent the nurse off for some tea. I was shaking at what he was going to say. He said my baby was very sick. The tea came. I sat looking into the cup. He said it might be meningitis.

My mother and I looked at one another in fear. That was very serious. The doctor said that he had to go back and do more tests, and would let us know as soon as he had any more results. Mam and I just sat there not knowing what to do. I just prayed.

'Dear God, please let my baby be OK.'

Time dragged. I paced up and down outside casualty. Up and down. My mother stood at the exit door smoking like a chimney. With our nerves in tatters, a nurse finally popped her head around the casualty door.

'It looks like we've caught it in time. Your son is going to pull through.' I sank into the chair with relief. It was only then I realised my body was shaking.

My heart broke when I saw him with the big clumsy drip attached to his little arm, but I was so happy and relieved to know that he would be all right. For two weeks I lived in Temple St. Hospital, sleeping at night in an armchair by his cot. He continued to make a steady recovery. One day, while he was sleeping, I slipped out to the local chippers to get something to eat. It was the only time I left him alone. As I was putting salt and vinegar on the chips, someone tapped me on the shoulder. It was Robbie, Simon's cousin. He was a nice lad and, unlike Simon, had never been in trouble. I told him about Damien.

'That bastard Simon doesn't know what he's missing. Where is he, by the way?'

'I don't know and I don't care.'

'Well the last I heard was he's in England somewhere. You're too good for him anyway, Anna.'

We talked for another little while about unimportant things and I hurried back to my baby. He was sleeping peacefully. Robbie's words rang in my ears and I tried to drown them out. I had more important things to give my energy to. My son was getting stronger by the day. It was only a matter of time before he would be let home.

I remember clearly the day Damien was discharged. The sun was shining in the window of our kitchen as I headed to the hospital. As I walked down the corridor one of the nurses called out to me that the doctor had already been around and he was to be discharged. It felt like the sun was shining everywhere. I bought the nurses a big bouquet of flowers to thank them, before I got into the taxi to take my precious son home.

The weeks hurried by. We were soon into December. The shops started to fill with flickering lights and decorations and toys of every description. This would be Damien's first Christmas. Christmas … I thought back to last year when Simon walked from Skerries to see me because he missed me so much. How things had changed.

One day as I was returning from town after doing some Christmas shopping, I met Tara, Simon's niece, walking through the flats.

'Anna, Elsie wants to see you. Said it's important.'

I wondered what was wrong. I left the bags in the hall and collected my baby from my mother's. I would bring him with me. Elsie hasn't seen Damien yet and I knew I couldn't go without him.

I climbed the flights of steps in Elsie's block with my bundle in my arms. I knocked at the now familiar green door. Elsie answered, her outstretched arms ready to greet me.

'Come in lass, come in. My, isn't he a bonny baby. I've been dying to see him. I thought you'd have come up to see me when he was born, you know? Though I can understand why you didn't.' Her eyes misted over for a minute. 'Let me look at this fella. Isn't he only gorgeous? He's just like Simon when he was a baby. I bet he's eating you out of house and home.'

'There's no feeding him, Elsie.'

'I'll put on the kettle and we can have a cup of tea. There's something I want to talk to you about.'

I watched as Elsie busied herself fixing the two cups and sneaking her favourite treat of the day from the cupboard – her Maltana. Elsie loved her Maltana. As I knew, only the welcomed visitors received a slice.

'You know Simon's gone to England, don't you?'

'So I heard. Maybe he might make a better go of things over there than he did here.'

'Well I hope so, love. He was only getting himself into trouble here with those fellas he was hanging around with.'

With the tea poured and Maltana cut, Elsie sat down.

'Now here's what I want to tell you. Before he left he was putting a couple of bob every week on a pram for you. He didn't manage to pay it all, so I'm going to put the rest to it. Celia is coming down and I want you to go up to the shop with her and collect it. Is that all right?'

'Well, I don't know what to say, really. I haven't got a pram and I do need one, but I'd say my mother'll go mad if I take anything off him.'

'Look child, don't you need a pram? That's the least the fecker can do for you, now isn't it?'

'Yeh, I suppose you're right.'

'He left a few little things in his room for you before he went away. I'll have a look for them now.'

As Elsie went off to Simon's room I heard the hall door open. It was Celia. She hadn't seen my baby either. She was all over him.

'Is this the little man, then? He's the image of Simon when he was a baby. He wanted to go up to see you at the hospital, but I told him not to. He was heartbroken over you. He was staying with me before he went away. Did you know he was gone to England? He's a job with Pat over in London.'

'If it's alright with you, Celia, I don't want to hear anymore about him.'

'Baba ba … who's a lovely boy then? It won't be long until he's walking.'

Elsie came back and handed me a plastic carrier bag.

'They're the things he left for you, Anna.'

I delved in to see what it held. Two cuddly teddy bears, and another soft toy with the inscription 'I LOVE DADDY', printed on its t-shirt. I didn't know what to feel. Before I could pull myself together, Celia was on at me to get a move on.

'Anna, are you ready now to go to the shop and we'll see about the pram?'

'OK so.'

'Make sure you come up to see me again, Anna, and let me know if you like the pram.'

'I will, Elsie and thanks.'

'Goodbye, my little man,' she said, as she planted a kiss on Damien's forehead.

On the way to the shop, Celia started her conversation about Simon again.

'I thought you two would get back together again as soon as the baby was born.'

I looked her straight in the eye.

'Celia, will you stop annoying me about him? It's over between us and that's the end of it.'

'Well, I hope you like the pram. He brought me in to show me the one he picked out for you.'

Inside the shop, she handed over some cash and a docket to the assistant. He went off to the storeroom and came back hauling a huge box. He cut open the flaps and I looked inside, the pram was grey. Not my favourite colour.

'Celia, I don't like this one.'

'Why not, isn't it grand?'

'No, it's not. I don't like the colour. I want a different one.'

I didn't know if I was just being contrary because he chose it, but I wasn't going to put my baby in a grey pram. Life was grey enough as it was.

The assistant overheard me and had no problem with me changing it.

'Pick anyone of those there,' he said pointing to the right-hand side of the shop.

I chose a navy 3-in-1 pramette.

I made up a little bed with the blankets I had with me and placed Damien inside to the relief of my aching arms. Then wheeling my baby in his new pram, I walked home, Celia still by my side.

'Why didn't you like the grey one Simon picked?'

'I just didn't, OK?'

Finally she got the message.

On reaching the flats, Celia offered to lift the pram up the stairs for me, but I refused. I didn't want my mother to see me with her. She still hadn't forgotten their last confrontation and neither had I. The only reason I went to the shop with her was because Elsie had arranged it that way. I was really pleased with the pram but I knew my mother would feel differently.

She answered my knock at the door.

'Where did you get that?'

Her voice was angry.

'Mam, it's not what you think,' I said pushing the pram into the hall. 'You know I went over to Elsie today. Simon was leaving some money off a pram during the summer before he went to England. Elsie paid the rest of it because he didn't manage to finish the payments. She gave me some teddy bears as well that he left for Damien.'

'The cheek of him. Does he think this is going to pull up for all the wrongs he's done?'

'Look, Mam, he's gone now, and I needed a pram. Elsie said it was the least the fecker could do for me.'

'Huh.'

Santa Claus came to my mother's for the first time in many years that Christmas, and brought much joy to the Mahon household. Opening his presents brought a memorable tear to my mother's eye and filled me with a great sense of pride. I laughed when my mother recalled the incident of the toy piano. I was very young at the time and extremely excited that Christmas morning as I crept into the sitting room. There beside the hearth was my toy piano standing on its three plastic legs. Full of delight, I scrambled up the stairs in the flat to show my mother my surprise. When I reached the top step I was exhausted; I let the piano slip from my hands and it promptly bounced back down to the bottom, tinkling notes as it went. How I yelled and woke up the whole house. We also remembered the year our Tommy hung up his stocking. He was sixteen at the time and after much taunting from me (his little sister) that he would get nothing from Santa, decided that by hanging up a stocking he would get back at me. Tommy was always teasing me. Six years between us he used to say that I was adopted and that really made me mad. However, I got the last laugh. Next morning Tommy discovered there really was something in his stocking after all, a rotten potato and a ha'penny.

We didn't have much as young children, but what little we did have we made the most of. Now here I was playing Santa Claus to my own son in the same familiar surroundings.

Mam went to great lengths to make the day as memorable as possible, but with the Christmas dinner and cracker pulling over, I began to feel a little sad. Another year was soon approaching and I had no idea of what it was going to bring. After Stephens's Day, Mam said she would babysit so that I could go out with Lisa. We went for a drink in one of the hotels in town. As we were sipping our drinks, a fella and girl passed by. The fella handed me my handbag telling me to mind it in case someone ran off with it. I thanked him and it was only when I went to pay into the nightclub that I realised he had robbed me of my few bob. That just seemed to sum up my life. I had gone out to try and escape the responsibilities of having a baby. I was looking for a little bit of distraction, and when I got the opportunity to go out I drank to forget. I started going out more with Lisa and her friends and drinking more too. Most nights I ended up in tears and my nights turned into drinking sessions. My thoughts drifted far away across the Irish Sea.

When New Year's Eve arrived, I went off celebrating with Lisa and ended up drunk towards the end of the night. Somehow we made our way to Christchurch Cathedral in time to hear the bells ring in the New Year. As we stood there being jostled by the large crowd that had gathered, a fella strolled up to me and asked for a New Year kiss. I looked at him and shook my head. It had nothing to do with him, I just didn't want to kiss anyone. But he wasn't pleased with my refusal. I gasped at the sudden pain I felt from the kick in the shin that followed. Tears sprang to my eyes as the bells started to chime. The bells were still chiming when trouble broke out; bottles started flying across the night air, there was the sound of breaking glass. The fighting had started. The guards were called and sirens screeched through the sound of the bells as they tried to break up the riots. Debris and glass lay strewn on the surrounding streets. In the distance I could hear the sound of ambulance sirens.

We were ringing in 1985.

I still continued to accompany Lisa on her nights out. I was looking for an escape route from my responsibilities and foolishly chose alcohol as my exit door from reality. I was lonely and very unhappy. I had a number of meaningless one night stands, but no sexual encounters. Whenever a fella asked for a second date, I either stood him up or I declined the offer. I was in a rut and my life was going nowhere.

It was during this downhill slide in my life that a knock came to the door. I couldn't believe who was standing there in front of me. It was Tony. It was almost three years since our last meeting. We stood staring at each other. It took me a few moments before I could speak.

'What are you doing here?' I said.

'I was just passing and thought I'd pop up and see how you are. Are you surprised to see me?'

'Surprised is not the word. I'm shocked.'

'Always said I'd stay in touch.'

'Come in, Come in,' I said, still dazed by his arrival. I knew my father was gone to the pub and wouldn't be back for some time, so it was safe to welcome my visitor. Inside I introduced Tony to my son.

'You … a baby. I know this is going to sound really stupid, but how? Who's the father?'

Before the questions started to swamp me, I filled him in on my life with Simon.

He took my son in his arms.

'God, he's big, isn't he?'

This was my life now, I told him. I asked him about his exams. He had done well and was hoping to go to the States when his passport came through.

We chatted for an hour or two until it was time for him to go.

'I'm going to be in town tomorrow, do you fancy meeting me?'

'Yeh, sure. The GPO at one?'

'OK, See you then.' I said, as I closed the door behind him.

That night I lay in bed thinking. What a shock it was to see Tony again. He hadn't changed much, his hair was a little shorter, that's all. He still had that cute smile. My life would have been so different if I had stayed with him. I could even be off to the States at this stage. I liked Tony but that's as far as it went. Someone else was still very much on my mind.

We did meet the following day. We went for coffee. We talked. We shopped. We laughed, had fun and then we said goodbye.

CHAPTER 8

It didn't take me long to realise the enormous amount of responsibility that a new baby brought to my life. There was baby food, clothes and nappies to buy now, bottles to make, nappies to change and a baby that need my attention every moment of the day. Soon it became too much for me. I was out on the balcony one day hanging up babygros when it just hit me. Tears came to my eyes. I sat on the ground and cried and cried. My mother had taken a part-time cleaning job to help out with the cost of the new arrival. She was doing everything she could to help me, but my da never missed the opportunity to get back at me. Whenever he had one too many, he'd shout out the windows of the flat, 'she's no fucking use.'

Living in the flats you could always smell the bacon and cabbage on a Sunday morning. Frank Sinatra singing 'I did it my way' could often be heard blaring from next door. I enjoyed growing up in the flats when I was younger. The boys liked to play 'Gestapo'. This was a game of chasing and if you were caught you were tortured and put in the den. The girls played *Queen-i-o who has the ball, Stuck in the Mud* and skipping. The Osmonds were our idols, especially Donny, but we liked Marie too, and we'd often sit on the swings and sing *Paper Roses* at the tops of our voices. Sometimes when I walk up the stairs and look out the side window that faces onto the playground, I think of us when we were kids singing on the swings and I smile. Stephen's Green was like our back garden and manys a happy day I spent there feeding the ducks. I always knew that's where the hippies hung out. I heard stories of them taking tablets and I was told they were to be avoided, so we left them to their own devices and kept out of their hang-out spots. But at seventeen, I was becoming aware that drugs were starting to affect the area in which I lived. I knew drugs were bad, I didn't know what they looked like, didn't want to either. But stepping over spaced-out drug addicts and syringes on the stairs of the towers was becoming a regular occurrence. Except these young people were people who I grew up with; they weren't hippies.

Crime was rising and every evening you could almost be guaranteed to hear one or two women screaming at the back of the flats 'He's got my bag.' Bag snatching and syringes had replaced the childhood games. I knew there were a few using the drugs in our blocks. Frankie in the next block was one of them. Nice poor fella; his mother used to be worried sick over him. She used to say 'He never has a butt and I hate sending him for ten smokes because then I mightn't see him for days. He'll meet some fella on the drugs and he'll be gone.' But she loved Frankie, and flowers too. She'd scrape up the makings of a dinner somewhere and then she'd buy a few daffodils to put on the table. So she was delighted when Frankie brought home a plant.

'There you go, Ma that's for you.'

'Ah, thanks, Son.'

'Now put it on the balcony and give it lots of sunshine.'

Two weeks later the flats were surrounded. A knock came to her door.

'This is the Drug Squad. Mrs. O'Dwyer. Do you know you've been growing cannabis on your back balcony?'

God, I laughed when I heard that story. Poor Frankie, he's dead now. Cannabis was the least of his worries. It was heroin that became the scourge. Most of the teenagers in the neighbourhood were using some kind of drugs, and the majority were using heroin. Parents' groups became widespread across the city concerned for the safety of their families. They refused to sit back and watch their communities be destroyed by this epidemic of growing drug abuse and violence. All-night vigils were commonplace by both mothers and fathers alike. In some areas they congregated around burning braziers in large groups, before staging protest marches on the homes of well-known drug pushers. Neighbours complained daily about syringes left scattered on the stairs. The darkness the towers offered became every junkie's paradise, a haven for their 'Fix'. We found ourselves constantly stepping over bodies stretched out on the concrete steps as we made our way to the local shop, the smell of Jeyes Fluid filling our nostrils as we went. 'Pushers Out' was the 'in' graffiti of the decade.

Life at home now was becoming more and more unbearable. My father's drinking was as bad as ever and it was taking every penny he got from the labour exchange. Things got worse when uncle Ernie came home from England. Daily my father and Ernie set off to the pub, and each night my father returned legless to hurtle abuse at me and lecture me on the immorality of my ways. On hearing Ernie calling from the flats one lunchtime, my mother opened the door and signalled him to come up. She was furious. She knew it was labour day and Ernie was calling to help my father spend his dole money.

'Come up. Come up. I want to see you,' she called. Behind her stood my father shaking his head and waving his arm, giving Ernie the message to carry on his way. I came down the stairs as this was all going on.

'What are you making hand signals behind my mother's back for?' I said to him.

'Get in you and mind your own business,' he roared. Ernie went off and the door was closed.

Inside my mother was saying, 'Don't be having him calling to the place. Coming up to spend your labour money, is he?'

With that my father clenched his fist and held it up to my mother's face. I rushed over and pulled her away, then stood in her place.

'Don't you ever raise your hand to my mother again. If you're going to hit anyone here, hit me! Go on put it there.' I pointed to my face. With my mother tugging at my arms, he withdrew his fist.

'I'll go where I like and when I like,' he roared and stormed out the door. It was the first time I ever saw my father, drunk or sober, raise a fist to my mother, and I made sure it was the last. I told my brother Tommy when he called up that lunchtime. It was the usual hour break he had from work at the wholesalers, except this time there was no time to eat; he spent it all searching the pubs on the street for my father. On finding him in Flanagans, he called him outside and issued him with a warning.

'If you ever raise a hand or fist to my mother again, I'll break every bone in your body.'

A couple of nights after that outburst my da fell in again drunk. He started on me the minute he came through the door.

'You, you fucking bitch. It's your fault, all of this. You're no fucking use, you and that bastard you were with. Ignorance and education how are ya?'

On and on he went that night, but the final straw came when he went out to the balcony and screamed, 'she's no fucking use, no use.' I sat and listened to his abuse until I could take no more. That was the last time I was going to hear him say such words against me.

'So you think I'm no use, do you? I suppose you think you've been the ideal father. You were no father to me. You're always in the fucking pub and then you fall in legless. Don't think I forget the times me and my mother had to go searching for you in all the pubs because there wasn't a crust of bread on the table. I don't forget, and another thing how dare you deny me an education. Instead of being proud of me, you slap that in my face the minute you fall in the door. I don't forget and I never will.'

'Don't you dare talk to me like that! Get out of this house!'

'Don't worry, I'm going.'

Quickly I grabbed a black refuse sack and bundled some clothes into it. Mam was watching me.

'What are you doing? Where are you going to go?'

'Mam, it doesn't matter. He told me to get out, didn't he? So I'm going and I'm taking Damien with me. Anyway, I just can't stay under the same roof as him much longer. I have to get out before he drives me crazy.'

'Look, he didn't mean it. He's just drunk that's all.'

'Drunk that's all. When is he ever sober?'

I picked Damien up in my arms, threw the bag over my shoulder, and left the flat, crying. As I said goodbye to my mother, my father didn't move from his armchair. I walked down the stairs, Damien weighing heavily in my arms, struggling with the awkward sack of clothes, my worldly goods. Where was I going to go? I stopped on the stairs to think for a minute. Jacinta's. Her mother wouldn't mind. I'd go to Jacinta's. I went around to the next block of flats and climbed the stairs. I explained the story to Jacinta and her mother.

'Sure, you can stay until you get things fixed up, love. Don't be worrying, everything will be fine.'

I spent a sleepless night on Jacinta's sofa, and the following day I set off up to Sandra's to see if they would put me up. She and her husband agreed to let us stay as long as necessary, and so I settled into their place. However since there were only two bedrooms we were very cramped for space. There was no room for anyone to move, so after about three weeks I had to eat my words and Damien and I moved back to my mother and father's flat. Mam was glad to have us back again. The relationship between my father and me returned to normal, in that not a civil word passed between us. The rows continued. The days turned to weeks and I was very unhappy.

CHAPTER 9

'Anna, Simon's home from England and he'd like to see you. Will you come over to Elsie's?'

It was Mags. I was gobsmacked at Simon's sister's sudden appearance at my hall door. 'What does he want to see me for?'

'Just wants to talk, I think. Sure come on over and have a cuppa tea with Elsie anyway. She hasn't seen you in ages.'

'Mags, I'm going out tonight.'

'Can't you drop over on your way?'

'Oh, alright so.'

Simon had been gone four months now and I couldn't help but feel a little curious about him, to say the least. Maybe the break away from that gang of fellas he was hanging around with did him good. The new navy suit Sandra had made for me that Christmas lay on the bed, ready and waiting for me to slip into before going out with Lisa and her friends. I took my time getting ready. My confidence needed a boost and I wanted to look my best when I met him. I went downstairs and told my mother that I'd be late home and took the key so I wouldn't disturb anyone when I came in.

I walked up the four flights of steps to Elsie's flat. The smell of Jeyes Fluid hung in the air. I was so nervous as I rang the bell and waited. A large shadow passed the kitchen window. My heart started to pound, my mouth went dry. The door was opened wide, and there he stood. Neither of us said hello. He followed me as I walked on through the hallway, into the kitchen.

'Hi ya, Elsie?'

'I'm fine, lass. What about yourself and Damien?'

'We're grand.'

Simon stood there hanging on to my every word.

'Would anyone like some tea?' he asked trying hard not to let me see him looking at me.

'I'll have one,' said Elsie. 'What about you, Anna?'

'I'll have a cup, but only if he's making it.'

'Right so,' he said, a little embarrassed by my last comment and went off to the kitchen to boil the kettle.

'You know,' Elsie continued, when he was gone, 'I got a great surprise when I opened the door and seen him standing there. I didn't know he was coming home at all. Doesn't he look well? He was doing a bit of work over there. Between you and me, he told me he missed you something terrible and he's dying to see the baby.'

Simon appeared carrying the cups.

'You're looking very well, Anna. How's my son?'

'Getting big.'

'I'd really love to see him.'

I heard the pleading in his voice. Some part of me felt sorry for him, and I gave in.

'Well it's too late to see him this evening, but I could bring him up tomorrow. Will you be here?'

'Yeh, I'm only here to see Damien.'

'I have to go now. I'm meeting someone at eight o'clock, but I'll be up tomorrow with the baby.'

I rose and headed for the door, Simon walking behind me.

'You're going out tonight then?'

'Yeh. Just a few drinks.'

'I don't suppose you'd fancy coming out with me?'

'Eh,' I turned to face him. He was still as handsome as ever, standing there in his stonewashed jeans and denim shirt. He looked far better than the last time I saw him. Gone was that dazed look.

'No strings attached honest. Just to talk, Anna.'

'Alright then.'

'Hang on until I get my jacket.'

Forgetting that I was meeting up with Lisa and her friends, we went into town that night to Boggie's Bar and had a couple of drinks. Later over dinner he told me all about London life, and desperately tried to catch up on all the happenings of my life in the past year. He asked me lots of questions, especially about Damien and the birth. He blamed himself for our break-up, and apologised the whole night long. He told me how much he wanted to be there at the birth and how it was his fault that he wasn't. He said he left for London when Damien was born to get a job and keep out of trouble, but how he always longed to see his son. It was this longing that had brought him home, and now he was nervous and excited at the thought of their first meeting. He said he was heartbroken when we split up, and that he was still madly in love with me. The night ended well, with Simon leaving me home, holding me tightly in his arms to kiss me goodnight.

'Please come over early in the morning with him. I can't wait to see him and hold him.'

'OK.'

'And thanks for coming out with me tonight, it means a lot to me. Goodnight, love.'

'Goodnight, Simon.'

Slowly I walked up the nine flights of stairs to my mother's flat. Had my feelings for Simon returned? Or had they never gone away? Was I that wrong to let Simon see his son? And how was I going to explain all this to my mother?

The following morning when I awoke, my mother was already downstairs in the kitchen making the breakfast. I knew there would never be an appropriate time to tell her, so in between the cornflakes and toast, I nervously filled her in on Simon's return. She listened to me without interruption as I told her he was working with his brother in London, but it was when I said he was now a reformed character that she cut me short. There was nothing that would convince her of that.

'You know, I had seen better things for you,' she said with tears in her eyes.

How could I say to her that once upon a time I too saw better things for myself.

I called to Elsie's that morning with Damien in my arms. Simon again answered the door. His eyes brimmed with delight at the first meeting with his son.

'God, the size of him. What have you been feeding him, Weetabix? Oh Anna, he's beautiful. He's so big. I can't get over how good-looking he is, he's just like his father. Let me hold him.'

He took Damien in his arms and bounced him on his knee. I was so happy to see them both together. I stayed for hours. We went out to the disco bar in Blooms Hotel that night and Simon told me he was still crazy about me. After another dance where he held me very close, he asked if I'd give it another go. He told me he was clean and he'd never touch drugs again. In the background Frankie Goes to Hollywood was singing *The Power of Love*.

So I did give it a second go for the short time he was in Dublin. Our happiness was short-lived, as Simon was soon to return to London again. We made the most of the time we had together, just the three of us. I bought him a chain and cross as a going away present. He was really surprised and promised to wear it always. When the day of his departure came we held each other one more time, tears streaming down our faces as we whispered goodbye.

Even though he had asked me to give him a second go, there had been no serious talk of reconciliation between us, nor had he promised to return or even to write from London. That was the way I wanted it to be. It was good to see him again and give him the opportunity to meet his son, but somehow I doubted if we were meant to be together, even though I had noticed a change for the better in him. London was obviously treating him kindly and I was glad to see he was on the right road again, away from the crazed drug scene of inner city Dublin in those early 1980s. Most of the teenagers in the neighbourhood were using some kind of drugs, and the majority were using heroin.

The days turned to weeks, and the weeks, months. A deep loneliness crept inside me. Even with all his faults, I missed Simon. I stopped going out with Lisa; Jacinta always seemed busy with her boyfriend and none of my school friends remembered that I existed anymore. Damien was my life now. Each day we went for walks into town or to the park. He enjoyed being out in the fresh air, kicking his chubby little legs and waving his arms at everyone and everything he saw. Sometime it was the strangers who stopped to talk and smile at him who were my only adult company in a long, cold day. It was when we returned from one of these walks that I heard Mags had called again. I could tell my mother was in a bad mood just by the look on her face.

'That Mags one was up here at this door looking for you. I told you not to have any of them calling for you. She said Elsie was sick. What I can't understand is why she's knocking here for you? She knows you have nothing to do with that family now, doesn't she?'

'I suppose she just wanted to tell me about Elsie that's all. What's wrong with her?'

'She never said.'

'I better go over and see, in case it's serious. I'd hate anything to be wrong with her; you know how well I got on with Elsie.'

I knocked at Elsie's door. Mags appeared.

'Elsie's in hospital. She had a stroke last night. She's in intensive care in the Mater.'

'Oh, God. Is she going to be alright, Mags?'

'I hope so. I haven't slept a wink all night worrying about her.'

'I'll go down and see her as soon as I check on Damien.'

I went back and told my mother what had happened. She took the news almost as bad as I did. Although they had never actually met and only knew each other to see, my mother had great respect for Elsie. She had listened to me time and time again speak about the kind-heartedness of this old woman, who had become my 'buddy.'

CHAPTER 10

On arriving at the intensive care unit I saw the family anxiously waiting their turn to go in and see Elsie. Ten heads turned and the talking turned to silence when I appeared. They were all there, except those in England.

'How is she now?'

'Well there's no change,' Jane said. 'She's still unconscious, but we're taking it in turns to be with her.'

'I'm next in,' said Tricia, 'but you can take my place if you like. You know we're going to have to tell Simon. Do you have an address where we can contact him, Anna?'

'No, I don't. Maybe Celia has?'

The doors opened and out came Celia and Angela, holding each other for support.

'I'll go in with you, Anna,' said Jane.

Feeling somewhat unprepared for what I was about to see, I entered the room. Elsie's frail figure lay motionless in the bed, surrounded by machinery that carried countless tubes into her body. Slowly I walked to her bedside and held her hand. A lump came to my throat. I could hear Jane mumbling some words on the far side of the bed. She was praying for her. I looked down at Elsie. Here was a woman who despite her 79 years had been so full of life and laughter. The tears filled my eyes as I felt the initialled pendant that hung around my neck. I wished so much for Simon to be here with Elsie right now. I left Jane by the bedside and went out into the corridor.

'She's going to pull through, isn't she Tricia?'

'We hope so, love. The doctors haven't said much, or given us much hope, all we can do is pray.'

'She looks so tiny in the bed.'

'Sure Mammy was always only a little woman. My Da is going mad with worry, there's no consoling him at all. He hasn't touched a bit to eat in two days.'

'I'll go over and see him when I get home,' I said.

'Celia has Simon's address in London and we were wondering if you'd write him a letter telling him about Mammy? Ask him to come home, love, he's needed here now.'

'Why don't one of you write to him instead of me?'

'You're much better at the writing, Anna, and we know if you ask him he'll be on the first plane.'

Celia handed me the address. 'It's urgent, Anna.'

Later that day, I wrote to Simon telling him about Elsie, and the family's wish that he come home. I posted it, and hoped it would find him as soon as possible. That night I couldn't sleep thinking of Elsie, and praying she would recover. Soon Simon would return again.

The days passed and Elsie's condition began to stabilise. Simon returned, anxious and upset at the news and began his bedside vigil. When Elsie did open her eyes for the first time, they soon began to water at the sight of her prodigal son. This time Simon promised to stay. She was in hospital for several more weeks. She had lost the power in her left side, and her speech was impaired. There was nothing more the hospital could do for her, and so they thought it best for her to return home. The family took it in turns to care for her; they worked out a rota of shifts. Often, I stayed over to help out and Damien stayed with me.

With Simon at home now and me involved so much with the family, it stood to reason that we would be spending a lot of time in one another's company. It was only a matter of time before we decided to live together. My mother didn't take this news very well. She was very angry at the idea of me 'living in sin'. Not alone that but 'living in sin with Simon' was the ultimate insult. Her opinion of Simon was unchanged.

'You're moving in with him? Anna Mahon, have you lost your mind? You know he's no good.'

'Mam, you know it's time for me to leave. At this stage, I've put up with enough of my Da; anything has to be better than living with him.'

Our first home together was a one-room flat in a dilapidated old Georgian house on Belgrave Square in Ranelagh. Simon's cousin, her husband and child lived on the bottom floor. Our room was on top of the house with a big old fireplace and even bigger old rickety window. A two-ring breakfast cooker and a table with one bench that Celia gave us was our only furniture.

It was Simon who found and rented the sparsely furnished room. I remember how thrilled we both were at having a place to call our own. Before we moved what little belongings we had into the flat, Simon picked me up in his arms and carried me over the threshold.

'Aren't we supposed to be married first before you do this?' I joked.

'Well you can't say you weren't asked.'

He dropped me on the bed and covered me in kisses.

'I know this place doesn't look that great, but it's ours and after a while we can paint it and buy some things to brighten it up. It's not much, but it's a start, Anna. Anyway I don't care where I live once it's with you and Damien.'

'You know Simon you're right, once we're all together nothing else matters. We can make this place really homely.'

'I love you Anna, and one day soon I'm going to make you my wife, that's if you'll still have me?'

Our first few days of living together were great. It was like we were a real little family and his past behaviour was forgotten as I played the happy housewife. I enjoyed cooking dinners for us and shopping for little treats when I could afford them. One thing that gave me great enjoyment was seeing our clothes drying together in front of the fire: his big shirts, my smaller blouses, Damien's little babygros. We were just like Daddy, Mammy and Baby Bear.

But it wasn't long before he developed this habit of disappearing without telling me where he was going or when he'd be back. There were so many days I spent alone with Damien wondering what time he'd be back for dinner.

One night when he came home after I'd just scraped another dinner into the bin, I flared up.

'Do you know I'm getting really sick of making dinners and throwing them out because you never come home on time? Why are you always so late?'

'Don't be annoyin' me about dinners; I'll eat them when I'm hungry. I had a hard time today with Max. I've had to listen to him all day giving out about the way the fittings were done on the job, and now I come in here and you jump down my throat. Just shut up and leave me alone,' he roared.

'Shut up and leave you alone, is it? Just who the hell do you think you're talking to? You're not the only one who had a hard day, you know? It's not all that great been stuck here in this crummy flat with no one but a baby, either.'

'If ya don't shut the fuck up, I'll put ya through that window.' He was standing now, fists clenched, his face filled with anger and aggression. Then there was silence. Minutes passed. I moved to the other side of the room and stood at the window gazing out across the rooftops watching the smoke bellow from the chimneys nearby. The door opened and then slammed. Simon had gone.

I was free to cry.

CHAPTER 11

It was after midnight when he returned. He was in a dazed state, complaining of exhaustion, the pupils of his eyes pinned smaller than usual.

'I'm sorry about earlier on, Anna. I didn't mean to say what I did.' He put his arm around me and was about to kiss me.

'Go away from me. What have you been up to?'

'Nothing, why?'

He swore blind of course he hadn't touched gear since he'd been back, and made up the excuse that he'd had a few pints with the lads before going over to Celia's to clear his head.

'Is that all right? I'm telling you I'm sorry.'

'Sometimes sorry just isn't good enough,' I stared into his eyes. He turned away.

'I promise I'll never say anything like that again. Look, I'm bursting to go the toilet. I'll be up in a few minutes.'

Down he went to the shared bathroom. I crept under the bedcovers hoping to get my night's sleep. But sleep wouldn't come. A long time passed before Simon appeared, moaning again of his exhaustion. What was he doing in the bathroom all this length of time, I asked myself? In the morning I'd have to go down and do a bit of investigating.

When daylight broke, Damien woke up crying for his feed. After breakfast, I quickly changed and dressed him, and carried him with me down to the bathroom, still not knowing what I was looking for or going to find. It looked much the same as it always did; nothing was out of place. There had to be something here somewhere, I thought. I searched behind the soap and bubble bath in the press, and found nothing. I got down on my knees and searched under the pipes at the back of the lavatory, still nothing. I pulled up the corners of the lino. I even looked in the cistern. What was I looking for? Anything that would give me a clue to Simon's behaviour. I stood and stared all around the tiny room, and then it dawned on me; if he was hiding something he wouldn't put it in a place where it could be easily found. Slowly, I pulled out the panelling that encased the bathtub. Surprisingly, I didn't have to use much force; it was already loose. I wasn't the first to have removed it. I looked inside and there I found what I was looking for, a small bundle wrapped in toilet paper with an elastic band neatly holding its contents in place. I un-wrapped the bundle, and there staring me in the face was my answer ... four empty syringes and an assortment of various sized needles. Horrified and angry, I picked Damien up and returned to the flat.

Simon lay in a deep sleep. He was drugged up to his eyeballs. I slammed the door and put Damien back in his cot.

'Get up, you lying pig.'

'What the fuck's wrong with you?'

'Look what I found in the bathroom,' I said, slowly producing the find from my pocket. 'Your precious needles. So that's what you've been doing in the loo half the night.'

I dropped the needles on the floor and stood on them. I threw the syringes at him. 'I'm sick of you and your lies and promises. This is not the life I want.'

He leapt off the bed and in a rage grabbed me by the throat and pinned me to the wall.

'You fucking bitch. Couldn't mind your own business could ya? Now you know I'm back on the gear. Are ya happy now? They're my fucking works right. What are you going to do about it?'

He released his grip and bent down to pick up his proud possessions.

'Ya bitch, you fucking bitch. You couldn't leave things alone, could ya?'

'I'm leaving and I'm taking Damien with me.'

'Don't you dare walk out on me.'

He swung round and clattered me right across the face.

'You aren't taking my son anywhere away from me. Do ya hear me?'

I didn't answer, I couldn't. When he turned to see why I wasn't answering him, he saw me lying on the floor; the force of the clatter had knocked me to the ground.

'Anna, I'm sorry, I'm so fuckin' sorry. I didn't mean to hit you. I didn't mean it. It'll never happen again. It's just that you annoyed me standing on the works. They weren't even mine. I was only minding them for a fella. Don't talk about leaving. I know I've been a right swine lately, but it's the gear, it's fucking up my head. I'll go to N.A. meetings again, anything, just don't leave me.'

He put his arms around me as tears streamed down my face. The pain I felt from his blow mirrored the pain I felt inside. I had wanted to prove my mother wrong about him, but now I couldn't. He had let me down and nothing he could do or say would change my mind. I had to leave but I knew he'd never let me walk out with Damien. In my heart I knew what I must do, wait until he was gone out. The day dragged. I became sullen and withdrawn. Simon showed no sign of moving from the flat. All day he spoke of how hard it was for him being at home again, meeting up with his old friends and how they were offering him gear whenever they met.

'I'm not strung out, Anna; honest, I can give it up.'

His words fell on deaf ears.

My chance finally arrived when Simon said he was going out to meet Max that evening. Once I was sure he was gone, I put Damien in his pram and left. I went home with my head hung low. When I knocked at my mother's door, she was both relieved and happy to see me again.

We hadn't seen much of each other since I moved out the week previously. A week; that's all it had lasted. It felt like a lifetime with all that went on. She welcomed me in her usual cheery way. I told her she was right. I should've listened to her.

'I'll put on the teapot and we can have a cup of tea. Your da's not in, he went off this morning. My God, what happened to your eye?'

'I don't want to talk about it now, Mam.'

A knock came to the door.

'I hope that's not my Da back or himself looking for me already.'

My mother went to answer it; it was my brother Davy.

'How are ya, Anna? Any tea, Ma? What the fuck happened to your eye? Did he do that?'

'We had a row last night. I'm not going back.'

'Too right you're not. Where's your stuff?'

'It's still up there.'

'That bastard. Right, that's it. Get your coat. It's time to sort this out once and for all. Come on, I'll go up with you and get it. I hope he'll be in when I get there because nobody, but nobody, does that to my sister.'

'Now, Davy you don't go getting yourself into any trouble. Do you hear me?' my mother warned. She knew her son of old and was aware how much trouble he could get into if he didn't control himself.

When we reached the steps of the house in Belgrave Square, my brother pushed open the door to the flat. No sign of Simon. The room was empty.

'Get whatever belongs to you and come on. Would he be down with that cousin he has living here?'

'He could be.'

I gathered the little I could find.

'I'm going down to knock. Which door is it?'

Down the stairs we went. I stood back and pointed at the door. He knocked. Simon's cousin Julie offered a friendly welcome and gestured us to come in. Simon was sitting in the armchair.

'Right you. Did you do that to my sister's eye? Get up.'

Simon didn't move.

'I'm talking to you. Did you do that to my sister?'

'I'm sorry, Davy, it was an accident. I didn't mean to hit her.'

'An accident. Some fucking accident. Get up off that bleedin' chair. Stand up and fight like a real man.'

I grabbed a hold of Davy.

'You promised me there'd be no trouble. Don't hit him, Davy.'

'Don't fucking hit him. Is that what you said?' Simon wanted to know.

'Davy, stop it. I only came here to get my stuff and go.'

'Well go on then; get your things together.' Simon smirked from the chair.

He was obviously happy to see me go.

Quickly, I went upstairs to what was our home for such a short while and gathered the rest of my belongings. I took everything I owned and left the room almost bare. I even unpegged Simon's clothes from the washing line and I packed not only the pegs but the line too. Then I just closed the door. In my hand was one of Damien's teddies and on it was inscribed 'World's Best Dad'. I hung it on the doorknob. I went back down to where Davy was. He stared long and hard at Simon, who still hadn't moved from the armchair.

'If you ever lay a hand on my sister again, I'll kill you. Now she's leaving here and she's not coming back. You're to leave her alone and don't be calling to my mother's for her either.'

Chapter 12

I moved out of my parents' flat in the summer of 1985 and into another one-roomed flat in Thomas Court. I was eighteen. This time it was just me and Damien. Set in the old tenement houses at the back of Guinness's Brewery, the room offered very basic living. The rent was £15 a week. My room was on the ground floor and measured 14 foot by 12 and had a small open fireplace and a bed. The two rooms across the hallway were vacant, while a young couple and child had just moved into the next room down the hall. The upstairs rooms belonged to an old man whose wife had died. There were no washing facilities, only a communal toilet and a Belfast sink out in the yard with one cold water tap. Washing clothes was a hard day's work and involved carrying pots of cold water from the yard into the flat and heating them on the two-ring breakfast cooker, washing the clothes in a big bucket and rinsing them again in the yard sink. I hated wash-day. So when I got a second-hand twin-tub it was like a dream come true. The whole street knew when it was my wash-day, as I had to put the hose out the window to empty the machine, and the sky filled with bubbles that could be seen floating all the way down the street.

I went out and bought a few rolls of wallpaper to brighten up the room – cream with blue flowers. Thomas St. was a great area to live near, with Frawleys, The Bazaar Market and the Liberty Market in Meath St. there was always a bargain to be had somewhere. On Saturdays the place buzzed with the fruit dealers, flower sellers and shoppers coming from all over the city. To this day the smell of hops and freshly-baked bread remind me of the time I spent there; Catherine's Bakery with its freshly made turnover and Guinness brewing their stuff over the wall. But night-time was lonely and a bit scary. Some nights I'd lie awake unable to sleep; other nights I'd be awoken by the sound of footsteps in the room above. Sure that room was empty, I had been told. I wanted to believe it was just my mind working overtime as I lay there stiff in the bed. But I could never be sure what went on above my ceiling.

Living in Thomas Court became very lonely after a while. I didn't have many visitors, so most days I went down to my mother's and came back to spend my nights alone. This became the daily pattern of my life. Damien was getting bigger, getting into mischief, and I needed another pair of eyes to watch him. My mother did everything she could for me and I would have been lost without her.

I was out shopping one day when I bumped into Simon. It was a hot summer's day and I hadn't seen him for a couple of months now. I'd heard he'd been down echoing the flats with his whistles, something that drove my mother mad over the years. I was surprised when he came up behind me and asked me where I was going.

'Home.'

'Home? Home where? You live that way,' pointing in the direction of my mother's house. He didn't know I'd moved out because she or I had never told him. He was amazed that I had a flat of my own and even more amazed when he'd seen what I'd done with it.

'Who did the decorating? I love the flowers on the wallpaper.'

At first he asked if he could visit the baby every now and then, but it wasn't long before he was spending a lot of time with us. And that was that. I was back to where I started. Though he didn't officially move in, he might as well have, he spent so much time there.

He was out one day and his niece Louise was minding Damien in the yard while I was trying to catch up on some housework. It was a warm evening. Suddenly she came running into the flat.

'Come quick, Anna, Damien won't stop crying and the man next door is after shouting over the railings to shut that bastard up.'

I ran out into the yard and picked up my child and settled him. There was no sign of the next-door neighbour.

'Just ignore him, Louise. Forget about it and don't say anything to Simon about this.'

With Damien happily playing with his toys and all quiet restored, I returned to my work. When Simon came back he was barely sitting down when Louise replayed the whole story. He turned on his heels and went back out again.

'I told you not to say anything, Louise.'

But she didn't know what all the fuss was about. She was too young to understand the implications.

He had gone next door and knocked on the neighbours. A medium-sized man answered. Simon's fist flew out at him. Bang.

'That's for calling my son a bastard.'

The first sniff of a fight and the whole street was out. Old men rolled up their windows and the women coming back from the markets stopped with their trolleys laden with toilet rolls.

'O Jaysus, what have you done now?'

A small crowd had formed a circle around Simon and the next-door neighbour as they eyed one another up. The coalman on his horse and cart pulled up and behind that a garda car. When they saw the garda car, some of the women got out their sweeping brushes and began to sweep as if they were just passing the time of day. Out stepped the two Gardaí, quickly putting on their caps.

'Well, what's going on here?'

'He called my son a bastard,' Simon got in there first, 'so I gave him a box in the nose. Now, I'm sorry, officer, for hitting him but I was a bit wound up. You know yourself, if anyone called the currant bun a bastard. He seems to have lost his contact lens, so me and the women here are helping him find it.'

He put out his outstretched hand to shake that of the neighbour's.

'Well, if you want to shake hands, we'll forget about it this time.'

They shook hands, and the guards turned and got back into the squad car. Talk his way out of a paper bag, that fella.

As Simon walked away a voice on the horse and cart shouted, 'We'll have to call you the Boxer after this.'

The women searched for over an hour for the contact lens and never found it. The neighbour did however when he went to the hospital. It was lodged in the back of his nose.

That was just one of the minor things that happened during my time in Thomas Court. The biggest one was that Simon's drug habit began to escalate. It was when I was doing the washing-up one day that I noticed I was drying more kitchen knives than usual, most of which I didn't own. After a little investigation, I discovered Simon was borrowing butter knives from the neighbours' kitchen to break into my flat when I wasn't there, to have a turn-on. When I challenged him about it, he denied everything. Sure wasn't he in denial about even having a heroin addiction. The fights, the beatings and the denials continued. I was stuck in the middle of it again. I had to get help, so one day after another blazing row where he wrecked the flat and boxed me in the face, I took Damien and went into refuge in the Regina Coeli Hostel in Brunswick St. It was a very difficult thing for me to do, but my face hurt and my heart was broken. I decided I couldn't live with a drug addict who wouldn't get help and I was fed up with the violence and shit that went with it.

Regina Coeli was my first experience of life in a refuge for battered women. I stayed only one night in the prefabs at the back of the buildings and listened to the cries of other children and their mothers who sobbed throughout the night. But me, I wasn't crying. I was too busy getting sick.

'No, I can't be, not again.'

Regina Coeli was not for me. Conditions there were squalid and I told myself I wasn't one of those downtrodden women who lived in fear of their lives, and besides with what might be another baby on the way, Simon would surely get help now. I wasn't as desperate as the women I had met in my short stay there. My life was going to be different. I was so naïve.

I returned to the flat the following day to find Simon had been busy scrubbing. The place was shining but he wasn't in. Thank God, I thought, a bit of peace. I knew I loved Simon. I also knew that even if he loved me, he loved drugs more. I set about thinking how could I go about changing things. He needed help with his drug addiction or this was never going to work. Suddenly the window went up; Simon stuck his head in. This was the way he often got into the flat. He never had a key, said he didn't need one.

'Let us in, will ya?'

I opened the flat door.

'Where did you go to Anna. I was worried sick?'

'I went away to think.'

'Away where?'

'I just stayed in a friend's place. This is not going to work, me and you, with you on the drugs.'

'I know I want to change. I can change. Things will be different when we get out of this flat, and I get a decent job.'

It was obvious he was stoned. He walked up and down the small room, avoiding eye contact.

'Simon, look at me.'

'What? What do ya want?'

'Look at me. You're stoned. And I can't take it anymore. Do you hear me? You either get help or I'm leaving you.'

I had his full attention now.

'You're leaving me.'

'Yes, I've been sick all night and I think I might be pregnant.'

'Pregnant? You're serious? That's great news.'

'How would that be great news? Expecting another baby in this hovel with you strung out on heroin.'

'I swear to God, I'll get help.'

And he did. My tests came back positive. I was pregnant and Simon was over the moon. He became a registered drug addict and now attended a methadone programme in Jervis St. I saw change and hope. My heart lifted. This time it would really be different. My pregnancy progressed and I continued looking after our son who was getting bigger by the day. The methadone programme would hold our little family together.

He went out one day to the clinic and didn't return as usual. Night-time came; I went to bed but didn't sleep. Had something terrible happened to him or was he just off on his travels again? I heard a motorbike pull up outside the window. I didn't stir. A knock came to the window. I pulled back the curtain. It was a guard, helmet in his hand.

Oh, Jesus, Mary and Joseph. I ran to the door.

'Sorry to disturb you. Are you Anna Mahon?'

'Yes.' I was shaking. Guards never brought good news.

'Simon asked me to call down to you to tell you he won't be home tonight. He's spending the night in the cells. We picked him up earlier for outstanding warrants.'

'What? Outstanding warrants.' I wasn't very good at this stuff and didn't know what he was talking about.

'Just to let you know, he'll appear in the District Court tomorrow morning. Again, sorry to disturb you.'

He got back on the bike and drove off.

Simon was remanded in custody and later given a six-month prison sentence for his shady dealings. I didn't know where Mountjoy Prison was. I'd never been there, never had any reason to be there, so my first visit was awful. As the big steel gates closed behind me I was absolutely terrified. My heart was broken and when I got my visiting slip and walked down to the cubicles waiting to see Simon, all I wanted to do was cry. I wanted to hug him, kiss him, tell him what an eejit he was. Most of all I wanted to take him home. But couldn't.

It was during this time in prison that Simon was rushed to the Mater Hospital. His appendix had ruptured and he had to have emergency surgery. I went to visit him after the operation. He looked drained and was hooked up to a load of drips, but needles in his arms were nothing new to him. Two prison officers sat by his bedside.

'Lads, would you mind if I had a little bit of time with Anna. Don't worry I won't go anywhere,' he said as I sat on his starched bed.

'OK, but no funny business. Remember we're right outside.'

The door had only closed when he started. 'Anna, get me out of here.'

'What are you talking about? You're just after your operation. Look at you, for God's sake, drips hanging out of you.'

'I don't care, just bring up my clothes and I can get the fuck out of here.'

'Who do you think you are? Batman. How do you think you can escape when you can't even get out of bed and there are two prison ...'

'Look, I'll think of something; just bring the clothes.'

'No.'

'Fucksake, some bird you are.'

Things were bad enough without me being dragged any further into it. I wasn't going to do this for him.

Simon remained in the Mater for another week and was transferred back to prison.

The visits continued.

On one such occasion, he was in very bad form. I knew being in there was getting to him and nothing I could do or say could make it any easier. He started giving out to me saying he wanted more visits. That day I didn't feel up to his complaining, so as the tears came to my eyes I got up and walked away. I was almost due the baby and wasn't feeling very well going in, so leaving I was in more of a state. I got on the bus back to my mother's, paid the bus driver all I had for the fare. Three stops up, an inspector got on the bus and told me I had to get off since I hadn't paid enough. The walk to my mother's was endless and the pain unbearable. I was ready to collapse. I crawled up the steps of the tower block and banged down my mother's door, tears rolling down my face.

'What's wrong, Anna?'

'I'm in pain, sick, I have to go to bed.'

I don't remember very much about the next two weeks. I ended up in the Coombe Hospital, dehydrated and with a bad kidney infection. Arriving back to the flat there were a half-dozen letters from Mountjoy Prison inmates telling me how much Simon loved and missed me. Never one for letter-writing himself he got his mates to do it for him. The ever-loving girlfriend, I was there outside the big gates on the day of his release.

He came back to live with us again and things were running fairly smoothly between us. UB40 were playing in Dublin and tickets were scarce. I knew Simon would love to go, so I managed to get one and put it by as a surprise.

He was thrilled when I pulled the ticket from up my sleeve and sent him off with my blessings to the concert. That night as I watched a film on the telly, I felt the first pangs and twitches of labour. I went to bed and woke in the middle of the night. Simon was back from his concert.

'Wake up. This is it.'

'What's it?'

'The baby.'

No phone, no taxi, no bus. We walked to the Coombe hospital, Simon carrying my case of baby things. Duration of labour, 5 minutes it said on the chart. A beautiful baby girl with black hair was born. Simon was at the birth with tears in his eyes when the nurse announced he had a daughter. We called her Rachel.

We settled into a life with two children. It was now 1986 and the flat was getting smaller since Rachel arrived. The weather was rotten and I was often stuck inside not able to get down to the shops. When it rained outside it rained inside as well. The wallpaper hung off the walls. There were times we had to take the mattress off the bed to dry it at the fire before we could go asleep. Conditions were terrible at the flat, but life had got a bit better since Simon's release. We spent more time together with little or no evidence of any drug-taking. Then the letter arrived.

His sister Mags came to deliver it.

'Me Da told me to bring it down, says it looks all official in its brown envelope.'

'Anna, you open it. See what it says.'

'It's your letter,' I protested.

'You know I'm not great at the reading and writing.'

I opened it.

'It's from the prison services.'

My eyes ran across the words on the page.

'It says you've tested positive.'

'Positive for what?'

Mags made a quick exit.

'HIV.'

Simon and I just stood there, looking at one another in disbelief. As the door clicked shut behind Mags, I stood staring at words on a page I didn't understand. I felt like someone had kicked me in the chest.

'What does that mean, Anna? Does that mean I have AIDS? Am I going to die?'

'What would I know about it other than the fact that gay men in America have it?'

'But I'm not fucking gay. If I have it, I could've given it to you. You're gonna have to be tested down in Jervo. I don't care about meself. Fuck it, if I have it, I have it. Jesus. The kids, Anna, the babies; if I've given it to you or the babies, I'll kill myself. I will. I'll kill myself. I could never live with myself. Anna I have to go out. I can't stay in this flat. I'll talk to you later.'

'Did you know you were being tested for it?'

'No, they must have done it when I was in with my appendix.'

He headed out the door, not even closing it behind him.

Round and round the words went in my head, HIV positive, HIV positive … I felt the world had just ended. My mind wandered back to a TV programme I had watched somewhere months before. It was an American programme and the presenter was interviewing gay men with AIDS. Images of their skeleton faces were flashing in front of my eyes. Visions of ambulance men in space suits and pictures of black body bags came back to me. No, this was not happening to me. This was not real. I must be dreaming. But it wasn't a dream. I was numb and no tears would come. I felt my body go lifeless and that it was someone else who was living this life and not me.

I went to bed with the words HIV positive and woke with them. I prayed that this awful news would go away, but no matter how hard I prayed, it didn't. Simon was HIV positive and I didn't know what to do about it.

Back then a positive test was a death sentence. It was a new virus and little was known as to how it had evolved; stories were in the papers about how it had been transmitted from monkey to man in some jungle in Africa. I wasn't interested in how it was originally transmitted. All I was aware of was the fear everyone had, including myself, about the virus that caused AIDS and how society outcast those unfortunate enough to be infected with it. Also, Simon didn't want to know. A bit like his heroin addiction, he didn't have HIV either, so it wasn't up for discussion between us. I tried to put a brave face on it, but I knew I would have to have the test done myself. It was then I started to feel what real fear was.

I began to dread every knock at the door. Knocks at the door meant bad news. There were no visitors to call with friendly chat or to share a joke and have a cup of tea. I often felt as if the flowers on that wallpaper were going to swallow me up. It was during this time of depression that a knock came to the hall door. It was early morning and Simon was still in bed. With baby in one arm, I turned the knob and opened it. A young, studenty type man stood in front of me.

'Hello. I'm looking for Anna Mahon.'

I stood staring, wondering who the hell he was and what he wanted with me.

'I'm from the Department of Social Welfare. I'm here to check your claim for lone parent's allowance.'

I broke into a cold sweat. This was all I needed, I thought.

'Sorry, can you just hang on a minute 'til I put the baby down.'

I shut the door quietly and turned on my heel.

'Simon, Simon, get up. It's the welfare man at the door. You're not supposed to be here.'

'Fucksake where am I gonna hide?'

I picked up the two cups of tea I'd just made and put them in the drawer.

'I'll hide under the bedsettee.'

There was another knock at the door. I opened it again.

'Do you mind if I come in this time? I need to look around. And I want to see your pension book, please?'

I reluctantly handed him my green pension book. As I did Simon sneezed from behind the bed-settee.

Mr. Social Welfare went to investigate, and pulling out the settee shouted, 'There's a man under here.'

Talk about stating the obvious. If ever I wished for a little green alien to beam me up, that was the moment.

Out came Simon from his hiding place.

'I'm sorry, but I'm going to have to confiscate your allowance book. You have a man on the property.'

'Confiscate what? You're confiscating nothing,' Simon shouted at him.

'I'm sorry, sir, but you're not supposed to be here.'

'I'm the father of those kids. I'm a registered drug addict and I have AIDS. Now give her back her book.'

The young man looked like he had just been scalded. Returning the book quickly, and with a very scared look on his face, he rushed out the door. I never saw him again. I couldn't believe that Simon would tell a complete stranger his health status. He knew the fear that those few letters AIDS had in the minds of everyone, and he was right. Now I was waiting with fear in my heart. I was going to have my own test done.

CHAPTER 13

Christmas 1986 was a memorable time for me. I got three presents: my beautiful baby girl, Rachel, a house in Tallaght and a negative HIV test from Jervis St. hospital. I was 19 years old and over the moon. This result was a great relief to me as in those early years when combination therapies hadn't yet been developed, the future for anyone with an HIV positive diagnosis looked very bleak. It was still generally believed that it affected gay men only. There were very few infections seen in women in the US or in Ireland for that matter, so some part of me believed it couldn't touch me.

Because of its newness, scientists and medical people were still only coming to terms with it. Discrimination was rife around those who were positive, people believing that it could be contracted from sharing cups and plates, hugging or using a toilet seat. A lot of resources needed to be put into education and information before these myths would be banished, if ever. Simon had got it from his drug habit and we knew it could be transmitted sexually to me, but to date it hadn't, so we dealt with it as best we could – by ignoring it. Even when it was general knowledge that it could only be contracted through drug users sharing needles, blood to blood contact, through sexual contact, or mother to baby, the ordinary person in the street still shied away from someone who was positive. My negative result saved me from that prospect.

Simon was in denial about ever receiving that letter with its death sentence diagnosis and I wasn't much better myself; maybe we thought if we ignored it, it would disappear. As yet he wasn't displaying any symptoms, so out of sight, out of mind. I put my head in the sand as well and just looked forward to my move into the new house. Somehow I felt immune to this big virus with a little name.

A three-bedroom house on the Ballycragh Estate in Tallaght was to be our new home. It felt like a mansion coming from a one room flat. The kitchen was bigger than the flat I left behind and everything I possessed fitted into it: a bed-settee, a cot, a TV and a two-ring breakfast cooker. Those early days in Tallaght were spent living in the kitchen. I didn't bother to bring the twin-tub with me. Now that I had my house I vowed that before long I'd have a proper washing machine. Until that day, washing was done by hand in the bath.

When I was growing up in the flats, Christmas had never really felt like Christmas at all. My mother's youngest brother had died on Stephen's Day before I was born, so she hated decorations. I always wanted her to be happy at Christmas, but she never was. Anyway, there wasn't money for tinsel or trees, even if she did like them. I grew up without a Christmas tree, but Santa still managed to come and leave a present each year by the fireside. I remember making Christmas bells out of egg cartons and wrapping them in tin foil to stick up on the window. Now that I was grown up with my own family, the first thing I wanted for my new house was a Christmas tree. I wanted my babies to grow up surrounded by the things I never had. I managed to decorate it as best I could and we celebrated our first Christmas in our new house.

Simon knew some of the neighbours who had moved from town already, so he was in his element re-acquainting himself with people he knew from years ago. There was Maree and Tony, three doors down. They had one child and their house was beautiful. I knew, because Simon told me and spent most evenings there watching videos. I was annoyed that he spent his time with them instead of being with us but I could understand why, they had everything and we had nothing. I challenged him once about it and his reply was 'I'm only watching videos, not on fucking drugs.' I couldn't argue with that one. I was happy to have a house, watch the children grow and not have to worry about his habit. I eventually got my washing machine. Simon put a deposit on a lovely front loader and we paid it off week by week.

When the news of Elsie's death came, it was an awful blow to him. He sobbed like a baby. He had always called her his ma, even though she and Paddy were really his grandparents. To him they were Ma and Da and that was the end of it. They were a lovely couple and had doted on Simon as a child, giving him anything he'd ever wanted. He often told me of the time he found out they weren't his real parents. He was twelve at the time and his class was going on a school outing. The teacher got on the bus to do a role check and make sure all pupils were present for the big day out. He kept calling out the name Simon O'Neill, but no one answered to that name. Simon was the only Simon on the bus or in the class, but his surname was Byrne just like Elsie's. He never went on the trip. Instead he ran all the way to his grandmother's house to ask her why his teacher was calling him Simon O'Neill. It was then Elsie told him that Celia was his mother and O'Neill was her married name and therefore his surname. Elsie had taken him when he was a baby to rear as her own because Celia needed time to recover after the birth. He just stayed on with his grandparents after that and assumed his surname was the same as theirs. Simon said his world fell apart that day, and blamed that as the reason he went on drugs in the first place. I was never sure that his addiction could be put down to that. One thing I did know; he was always quick to blame something or someone else for his behaviour. After all Elsie and Paddy were devoted to him. If anything, it should have been a source of strength to him and not the other way around.

It was anyone's guess as to how he was going to deal with Elsie's death? I was worried sick. I knew how well he'd been doing up to this and I didn't want to see him slide back into his bad ways. I told him he had to be strong for Paddy. He'd need him more than ever now, now that he was without his wife whom he had shared over fifty years of married life with.

'You're right, Anna. He's not going to want to live now without me ma. We're going to have to go into town more to see Paddy. Bring the kids in to see him. You know, they both adored you.'

And I did know. I was heartbroken when Elsie died. She was such a character and, almost to the end, was still doing her wheeling and dealing over on the Hill on Dublin's northside. Early Saturday mornings she'd set off with her old pram full of second-hand bits that she had collected during the week from neighbours and friends: curtains, bedclothes, old clothes, toasters, irons, jackets and shoes – anything that she could sell to make a few bob. She'd set up her stall and tell her customers she had exactly what they were looking for and if she didn't, she'd get it for them the following week. Simon said she'd sell sand to the Arabs and he wasn't far wrong. A story goes that one of her own sons called to the flat with a pair of his old work boots so she could sell them on the Hill. By the time he was leaving she'd sold them back to him for a tenner.

Visiting Paddy in the flat after Elsie had died always felt wrong. I'd sit there in the silence expecting to hear her little voice say, 'will someone make us a cup of tea and give us a slice of that Maltana.' But Elsie's voice was to be heard no more, and Paddy sank deeper into the dark lonely pit of life without her. Within months he developed cataracts in both eyes and, despite an operation to save his sight, Paddy went blind.

Simon remained off the drugs after Elsie's death. Despite my fear that he would go back on them as a way of dealing with his grief, he was strong-willed and said that drugs didn't have a place in his life anymore. I was eager to believe him. There was no more talk of HIV. We went on with our lives as if that letter never arrived.

He found a new best friend, Tomo, and I often wondered if they were joined at the hip, because when you saw one you saw the other. Tomo lived with his family up the road in a corner house. Tomo's sister Caroline lived with her husband James at the back of our house. They had two small children, just like us. Caroline and I became good friends. We both knew what it was like to scrimp from one end of the week to the next with little ones to look after. We both got tic in the shop to tide us over and we'd sit cursing ourselves for having asked for more credit. Of course there were times when the bill in the local shop was too much and next week's money would be already owed out. Such was the poverty we lived in. We'd have nothing in the cupboards, yet our two houses would be gleaming. At times Caroline and I didn't have a crust of bread between us. I remember one time, things being so bad we made roll-ups out of a tea bag. Anything we had we shared, and whichever one of us thought we could make cigarettes out of tea bags was as crazy as the other.

Unemployment was high and most of the fellas that lived on the estate had no jobs to go to. So they set up a football team to beat the boredom. Tomo was desperate to get Simon on his side; Simon wasn't having any of it.

'Ah, Tomo come on, give us a break. I don't know when was the last time I kicked a ball.'

'Come on ya lanky fucker and don't be givin' me excuses.'

'I'm not fit Tomo. I'm not even a year off the gear.'

'All the more reason for you to get up and do something. Ya won't get fit sitting down.'

'I haven't any shorts, Tomo.'

'No excuses.'

Tommy went off and knocked back with a pair of shorts. Caroline and I went around the field pushing our prams waiting for the game to start and when Simon turned up there was a roar from the pitch.

'Here, Simon, you'd know those legs never saw daylight. They're like two milk bottles. I saw more meat on a butcher's pencil.'

It was the first match Simon played and despite the slagging, it was not the last. It was great to see him with a healthy interest. Tomo was good for Simon. He was the fun Simon needed. Harmless fun and life away from drugs.

For a while we played happy families. We had our house; we had two lovely children and we looked forward to watching them grow up strong and healthy. My whole life was ahead of me and HIV wasn't going to get in the way of that. We did take precautions most of the time. I was on the pill and we used condoms to prevent transfer of the virus, but I tended to get lax about using them from time to time. I was naive and thought I was immune to it. Simon was in denial still. I suppose I went along with him, because to look at him there was no sign of illness. In fact, with him off the drugs and taking healthy exercise like the football he was better than ever I saw him.

I already had my hands full with Damien and Rachel but then I started to suffer pains that lasted a number of days, and before I could do anything about it I collapsed in the hall. I don't remember how long I was there when Simon came in and found me. The doctor said I'd have to go to hospital straight away. At the hospital it was discovered I had an infection in my womb and was put on strong antibiotics and painkillers. This seemed to clear up the infection. However weeks later I found out that I was pregnant. No one told me that some antibiotics affect the pill and stop it from working. This time Simon wasn't happy.

'Jaysus, Anna, another baby. How are we going to manage? We can't cope with the two that we have. How can we go through all this again?'

The pregnancy went without any major hitch, but Simon was never happy about it. He complained all the time that we couldn't afford another baby. We went from day to day looking for credit in the shop until we had some money gathered together to pay it back, which never seemed to happen. The great hopes I had for Simon and his new interest in football began to fade away. He always seemed to be in a mood these days.

I was driven to the Coombe hospital by a getaway driver that Simon had lined up especially for the upcoming event and he crashed every red light from Tallaght to Cork St. on our way there. Simon dropped me at the hospital and left me on my own to give birth to Alan, barely an hour later. Like all my babies, Alan was beautiful. He wasn't dark like the other two, but had hair as white as snow. I wished his father could be there to see his gorgeous son, but that didn't happen 'til the next morning when he arrived up with a tracksuit for me for Valentine's Day. I didn't dare ask where he got it from, though it summed up my life, I thought. What man abandons the woman he loves as she is about to give birth, then turns up on the most romantic day of the year with a present of a tracksuit for her?

They kept me another few days in hospital. Simon spent more time in the visiting room, chatting to other visitors, than he did by my bedside. If I had my wits about me I'd have guessed that it wasn't swapping father stories they were doing. The football or his family no longer held him. He was back to his old tricks. He told me he left a deposit on a cot mobile but was short £20. He wanted to collect it on the way home. Like a fool I fell for it and handed over the money. Anyway I thought what could he get for £20?

My homecoming was another story. He told the taxi man that his wife had just had another baby, one we couldn't afford. The taxi man stared at him in horror. 'You should count yourself lucky, pal. Me and my wife could never have kids.' There was stunned silence for the rest of the journey. When we got home there was no talk of what had just gone on. It was as if it never happened. Simon set about making the dinner. He put mine on a plate and then threw it out the back door.

'You don't deserve any dinner,' he roared at me. I just couldn't believe that he could do something as cruel as that when I was just after giving birth and trying as best I could to look after my baby. I was in tears.

The honeymoon period was over. We were back to the bad old days with a bang. Family, football, a new son, were no competition for his habit. I didn't know what to do, so I turned all my attention to looking after my new baby and our other two children.

A new form of drug had appeared on the streets of Dublin – little grey tablets called MST's (morphine sulphate tablets) otherwise known as Napps. The grey ones were 100mg and Simon soon developed a chronic addiction to them. MST's are prescribed for pain relief to cancer patients, but Simon didn't care. I watched as this new habit took hold of him. Sold on the streets for £20, each of these little tablets proved an expensive habit to maintain. This time Simon was beyond help. He'd get up in the morning, go over to Ballyfermot to score his Napps and come back to cook them up. First he cleaned the grey off each tablet before crunching it on a spoon and adding a drop of water. Then he heated his concoction on the two-ring cooker, stirring it with the needle of his syringe. He'd wrap a belt around his arm, find a vein and inject himself to get his hit. I had lost my battle, and drugs had won. I didn't live with Simon anymore; I lived with an addict whose sole purpose in life at that time was running around Dublin looking for dealers so he could buy his wares from them. An addict who sank to all time lows to fund his habit, bringing me with him to the depths of despair.

A dealer on the northside was his main supplier and when Simon said he was too sick to get out of bed to score his Napps, it became my job to get the pick-up. The dealer was happy to have me call to his house. I was unassuming and wouldn't get the eye on him. A married man in his forties, he was much older than me and also much wiser; he'd wrap the tablets in a corner of a plastic bag and tell me to put it in my mouth until I got home. If I had been able to see into the future when I was sixteen and had seen the picture of a woman walking the streets with a plastic bag of tablets hidden in her cheek I wouldn't have believed it was me. Where had all those dreams gone when I sat in school and believed I was going to be a social worker? What a different path my life had taken? I knew what I was doing wasn't helping Simon but I was afraid. Somewhere along the way I had got sucked into his low life. I had now become an enabling factor to his addiction. Deep down I knew I'd lost him.

Returning one day with four Napp100's in my mouth. Simon was waiting in the kitchen with his spoon all ready for my special delivery. He started to work on his preparations. I turned and saw what he was using. The syringe had broken and furiously Simon had replaced the plunger with a five-inch nail.

'The bleedin' works is after breakin'. This thing better fuckin' work.'

He picked up the syringe with the nail sticking out, put it into his vein, pressed on it to go in and blood and morphine squirted into his face.

'That's your bleedin' fault. If you didn't throw out my old works I wouldn't have to use this. Now I've lost it. I've lost my fuckin hit.'

He grabbed me by the hair and hit me in the face. I fell to the ground.

'You go back over and get me another four. Tell him you want a lay-on 'til tomorrow and get me a barrel syringe. Do you hear me, you fuckin' cow. Don't come back unless you have what I need.'

Then he grabbed me and threw me out the door. I made my way over to the northside. I pleaded with the dealer to give me more tablets until the next day. Even he was shocked at the state I was in.

'Anna, I'm going to say something to you now, whether you like it or not. And for Christ's sake you're not to tell Simon.'

I wasn't interested in any conversation; I just wanted to make the collection and get out of there.

'Can you not see what he's doing to you? The state he has you in? You need to get away from him, Anna, before he kills you. Go anywhere, but get out of this. You deserve better.'

I was so shocked no words would come. I couldn't believe what he'd just said, words of wisdom coming from a very unlikely source, a drug dealer. He didn't have to say that. Drug dealers don't care who they sell to as long as they get their money. But this one did and I had heard his words.

'Soon,' I thought, 'very soon, but how? Where would I go? I had nowhere.'

I still had to get the barrel syringe and on my way home I pleaded with the man in the chemist to give me one. He must have seen the terror in my eyes when I told him I couldn't go home without it. He thankfully obliged and on the last leg of my journey I made up my mind I was going to leave my home. Home. What a laugh.

CHAPTER 14

On the 19th February 1991 I discovered two things. One, that I was pregnant again and, two, that I had the courage within me to leave. Simon's drug habit was totally out of control, and I had no idea what sort of criminal activity he was up to in order to raise the huge amounts of money he needed to feed his habit which was running at £1,000 a week. My life was very much in danger. I knew if I was to survive, I couldn't keep this up any longer, so when he got up that morning and went out, I told the children I was bringing them for a walk. I put on their coats, went out the door and didn't look back. With £10 in my pocket I got on the first bus that came. I didn't have a plan, didn't know where I was going, just hoped that somehow, somewhere I'd find another life. I had to search deep inside my very soul to find the strength to get away. I knew what I was doing was dangerous, leaving him like that. I also knew I was taking a big risk leaving because if it didn't work out, I'd have to come back to him.

'Who's going to make Daddy's dinner, now that we're gone?' Rachel asked.

'Daddy'll have to make his own dinner from now on,' I replied, holding her hand more tightly. I didn't know how much they knew of what was going on. Once Damien had seen him hit me with a flowerpot and when Simon had left the room, Damien picked up the pieces off the floor and hid them in the back of the cupboard saying, 'He won't be able to hit you with that any more, Mammy.' God, the innocence. The child thought he was protecting me from any more assaults. If only it could have been so simple. I know now that I must have had a guardian angel, someone must have been watching over me.

I don't remember arriving at the refuge for women and children in Rathmines or even how I found myself there. I just knew at the time that I had to get away and fast. I also knew that if I was to have any life at all I'd have to leave Dublin, and that's what I did. With the help of wonderful women in Women's Aid, I moved to another refuge outside Dublin and from there to a refuge in Galway.

Refuge is a safe place away from domestic violence, a room in a building that holds no fear. It's a sanctuary for tormented women, not weak women, but strong women whose lives are often driven to despair. This one had five families in similar situations to my own. My children and I were given one little room that had bunk beds with a tiny kitchen in one corner. But it didn't matter; we had a breathing space and everyone was very caring and very understanding.

I've met some of the most amazing women in the times I've spent in refuge. You go in not wanting to talk or share your life with anyone; you want to keep your business to yourself, but slowly you realise these other women are in the same situation as you, some worse than others. Like Nell. She told me she was adopted as a child by this farming couple. Her father sexually abused her for years, until one day when she was a teenager she ran away. Shortly after that she got married to another violent man who used to beat her senseless. She had five children when he signed her into a mental home. She managed to get out and found her way to the refuge. I'll never forget meeting Nell. She'd never had any money as the husband kept it, spent as little as possible on food and the rest on drink. Now he had her children and she was totally on her own. The first time I brought her to a supermarket, she ran back out because she couldn't get over the amount of food that was in the shop. Aisle after aisle of it. It was too much for her. When I bought her a pair of red shoes, she sat and stared at them for a week and wouldn't put them on.

Then there was Marcella, a woman who had two sons, but one had been killed in an accident and the other was in prison. Her husband drank whiskey all day, lashing out at her whenever the humour took him. I often came across Marcella in the laundry room crying, just standing there, crying.

Meeting them gave me the strength to keep going.

We had come with just the clothes we stood up in. I'd never been to Galway before and didn't know one street from the other. Often when I went to search out the charity shops for clothes that might fit the children, I'd get lost and have to ask for directions to find my way back, all the time looking over my shoulder in case I was being shadowed.

'Anna where the fuck are ya?'

That was my brother's response when I rang to tell him I was safe.

'Galway,' I said reluctantly, afraid even to tell my family where I was.

'What the fuck are you doing in Galway?'

'I had to get away.' And I put down the phone. That was what I had to do. Tell them as little as possible to ensure we were safe. I could take no chances where Simon was concerned. I felt very, very alone.

It was suggested that I should start the two older children in school. This was a big step for me. It meant I was here to stay. I wasn't going back. My first encounter with a school in Galway, however, wasn't a good one. That Monday morning the heavens opened and we were all soaked to the skin by the time we reached the school. I had tried to reassure them that they would be OK and that things would get better for us now. So stepping inside the big school-gate, I held their little hands as the rain ran down our faces and squelched in our shoes. The principal appeared – a big rough man with a scowling face. He knew we were from the refuge as we stood there dripping wet on his doorstep.

'You're not bringing those children in here like that,' he said and throwing a tea-towel at me, told me to dry them.

There was no good morning or how are you, nothing. As I caught the cloth I stared back at the ignorant man.

'Do you know something? We won't be needing your dishcloth because my children won't be going to your school.'

I threw the tea-towel right back at him, turned and walked out the door we had just come in. Outside I gave the children a hug and explained to them that there was one school they wouldn't be going to. The last thing we needed in our lives was a horrible person like that. I did eventually find another school run by a lovely nun who welcomed my children with open arms.

One day in the refuge I was told there was a phone call for me. Immediately my heart started beating. It thumped in my ears as I went down the hall towards the office. Nobody knew where I was. Had Simon found me out? What would I do if it was him? I picked up the phone nervously.

'Hello?'

'Anna, it's me, Sandra.' My sister had discovered where I was.

'God, you frightened the life out of me. I thought it was Simon. How did you find out where I was?'

'I guessed. Knew you were in Galway so I looked up the refuge's number and enquired about you.'

'Is there something up?'

'Paddy's died.'

A terrible sadness crept over me. I was very fond of Paddy, and now with both him and Elsie gone, the two most important people in Simon's life, I wondered how he was going to cope. With me and the children out of it too, there weren't many people around now who cared for him. All I could be sure of was that his one true love hadn't deserted him. Drugs. He must be in a very lonely place. Paddy's death was bound to affect him.

For my own safety, I knew I couldn't go to the funeral so I went to a church with the children and we each lit a candle for him. He and Elsie were a big part of my children's life when they were babies. Paddy used to collect the twenty pence coins for Damien. Even when he went blind he could tell the difference between the various coins by their edges. Going to the church was our way of saying goodbye to him and on the way back to the refuge we sang, 'don't worry, be happy.' That was Paddy's song.

I was on Social Assistance when I came to Galway first and that meant money was always in short supply. I had no shoes, the plastic runners I had were falling off my feet, so one Thursday I felt it was time to invest in a new pair. I knew they had to be cheap whatever I was buying. I eventually found a pair of sandals for a fiver. It didn't matter that it was the coldest month of the year or that sandals would give no protection from the biting Atlantic winds or even the fact that they were bright pink. The most important thing was that they were cheap. I was delighted with them. Beggars couldn't be choosers.

On Sundays the children and I would walk to the beach with a bottle of diluted Miwadi juice. We'd collect shells and make pictures in the sand and on a good day we might find a baby crab. I always told them not to hurt the crab; that he was only trying to find himself a home just like us. So Damien and Rachel would build the baby crab a home on the beach in Salthill. It was in this time that I learned how simple and peaceful life could be.

We spent almost two months in the refuge before I felt it was time to move on. I found a house set in a rural community sixteen miles from Galway City; a big farmhouse over two hundred years old, complete with its own barn in the back garden. This was to be our new home. I was now five months pregnant and wondering how on earth I was going to cope with a new baby living miles away from any family or friends. As time went by family started to come and visit us in our big old house. It felt funny at first because they had never really visited me in Dublin, but now that I lived in the country and I was away from Simon they became part of my life again. It felt good.

On one of these visits my father came with my mother. We hadn't talked for years but when I saw him standing there at my door I let bygones be bygones. We managed to get on and he was very interested in the garden and the old farmhouse which kept him occupied during his time with me. Neighbours passing used to see his shirts hanging on the line with the rest of the washing and thought I had a new boyfriend living with me.

I enrolled the children in the local national school. It was a whole different life to that of the life I had in Dublin and it was often reflected in my inability to communicate with the local people. I simply didn't know what to say or how to relate to normal living. One afternoon I was at the children's sports day when two women tried to engage me in their conversation; I just didn't know what to say. They were talking about curtains, but I sat there dumb while the two women continued talking above my head. They might as well have been talking about rocket science, their language was so alien to me. Curtains. What did I know about curtains or the everyday life they talked about? Now if they were chatting about syringes and the gear and how to dodge the blows from Simon's fists, I'd have been well away. But curtains!

Slowly things got better. I really enjoyed the walks with the children, bringing them out to see the sheep, the cows, the horses and hens. Damien was seven, Rachel had celebrated her fifth birthday, and Alan was three. I had wondered how they'd adapt to living in the country, but I shouldn't have worried. They enjoyed every minute of our time there, from feeding Smarties to the sheep, collecting farm eggs from the farmer up the road, to the day we watched the collie working with the sheep. The children were amazed by the way he responded to his master's whistles and cornered the flock in the field. All these were treasured memories right down to the splinters in their bums from sliding down the ladder in the barn. This was living. This was the life I had hoped to give them that day I walked out of my house.

I still had nightmares of Simon finding me. Waking up in the middle of the night was a regular occurrence, when the least noise would startle me, whether it was the wind shaking the trees outside or a book falling off a bed. To ease my mind I took up a new hobby – knitting. It was something I never knew I could do and the word spread around the village. A few of the neighbours knocked at the door to admire the baby clothes I had made, and some of them even placed orders. This was how I made friends with Deirdre. She was a retired midwife from Dublin living in the village, and she would often call for a friendly chat. All this did my heart good. Now that I had made up with my dad after all the years, he too had became another regular visitor.

When I finally went into labour that August all my family was there to welcome the new arrival, a baby boy I named Gareth. He weighed in at a healthy eight pounds, six ounces. The family fussed all around him, but when they left to return to Dublin I cried for days. I was so lonely. I was twenty-four years old, living in a farmhouse in the middle of nowhere with four small children. They were my life now and they needed me. We had nothing but each other. When they'd go to bed and I'd hear their laughter upstairs I'd remind myself I was alive and doing well. There were no arguments or violence now, just soft words, hugs and kisses. Hadn't we made it?

I didn't feel well after I had Gareth; I seemed to be picking up one infection after another. Dr. O'Brien only visited the village once a week and the nearest chemist was six miles away. Deirdre often gave me a lift to collect prescriptions and I was glad of her help. I don't know how I'd have got to the next town to pick them up otherwise. Those sore throats and fluey-like symptoms just wouldn't go away, the runny nose, the headaches, the sweaty sleepless nights. I knew these symptoms could relate to many other infections or allergies, but something was haunting me and it was time to face it again. It was time for me to make that appointment with Dr. O'Brien.

It was mid-November and bitterly cold the day I walked into his surgery.

'Ah, Anna. How are you?'

'I'm fine … fine.'

'And the baby? Sleeping OK now, is he?'

'Yes, he's fine too.'

Struggling, I was struggling but the words wouldn't come out.

'Doctor, I want to have an HIV test.'

There I'd said it.

'And what makes you think you need one?'

God help me get through this.

'Because my ex-partner was a drug addict and he was HIV positive.'

'And were you on drugs as well?'

'No, but we did have four children together.'

'I know it's a difficult question but how long is it since you had sexual relations with him?'

'About ten months,' I said counting back to the morning I walked out. 'Why?'

'Because the test measures antibodies to the virus and it can take up to three months for them to show in the blood.'

'And what are antibodies.'

'When the virus enters your blood stream, your body tries to destroy it. One of the ways it does this is by producing fighter cells to attack the infection; these are antibodies and that's what the test measures. We can take some blood today and send it off. But I'm sure you've nothing to worry about.'

'How long will it take for the results to come back?'

'About three weeks.'

And as he took out the syringe to take my blood, I turned away.

I'd done it, now all I had to do was wait. As the days passed I thought I was going to lose my mind. I'd no one to talk to about it. I know I had the test done before, but this time it was different. Over and over it went round in my head. What if I was positive, what if I got really sick, who would look after my precious children? What if, what if? The questions went round and round until I was barely able to function. I knew if I was to get through this I had to tell someone, and that someone was Deirdre. I thought with her being a nurse and a mother herself she might understand what I was going through. So I plucked up the courage and told her. She didn't bat an eyelid.

She was so kind offering to do whatever she could, especially minding the kids for me. After she calmed me down she brought them up to her house so that they could play on the swings. That evening when she came back down with them and we were having a cup of tea, she dropped her bombshell.

'Anna, I don't want to frighten you or anything, but I think you need to stop breastfeeding, because HIV can be passed through the milk.'

'Jesus, don't say that, Deirdre. Nobody ever told me that.'

It just showed how little I knew about the infection. I put my head into my hands and started to rock.

'Nobody told me.'

'I'm sorry, Anna. I thought the doctor would've talked to you about it. It's not fair that you should hear it like this.'

'What if I am positive and I've infected Gareth? I'll never be able to live with myself. I'm terrified, Deirdre. What will I do?'

'Anna, you'll drive yourself crazy. Stop. You have to try to keep yourself together, at least for the children's sake. Now let's just wait and see what the results are.'

And as she put her arm around me, I began to cry. I wished I could believe I had nothing to worry about. I was sorry I'd done the test at all now. Waiting was agony and having to abruptly stop the breastfeeding was even more painful. How is a mother supposed to feel, thinking that she could have given her baby contaminated breastmilk? That's what it would be, wouldn't it? Contaminated? Is that the right word? That's a dirty word. Sounds dirty, doesn't it? Contaminated. I was going mad with worry.

On the 24th November, 1991, Freddie Mercury from the band Queen, died from broncho-pneumonia as a result of AIDS. He was the first major rock star to have died from the disease. He had kept his status private until twenty-four hours before his death to protect those he loved and who loved him. The world mourned his loss. AIDS was in the media again. Every TV channel, radio station and newspaper carried news on the life and death of the great rock legend and how he had died from the virus. Meanwhile in a tiny rural village in Co. Galway, I was waiting on the results of a blood test that could change my life.

I had always liked Queen. I remembered the great performance they gave at Live Aid in Wembley Stadium in July 1985. *We are the Champions* was a particular favourite of mine. I remember how proud I felt of our Bob Geldof and thinking, 'imagine it took a Dubliner to organise that and help those starving in Africa.' Yes, I was very proud of our Bob and had watched along with millions of others as Freddie belted out the old rock classics '… And we'll keep on fighting till the end'. And he did.

I rang the clinic after two weeks and the results still weren't back. The doctor told me it could take another two to determine the outcome of the test. The waiting game continued. I was at my wits' end.

On the 13th of December, I found myself in the doctor's surgery again, waiting to be called. I was so nervous I wanted to get sick. My turn came and I went in. Behind a red curtain I could hear my doctor talking to his wife, who was also a doctor in the same practice.

'For God's sake, Ruth, How can I tell her?'

'You have to, because you're her doctor.'

'But she's only a young woman and she has young children?'

'Look, just go out there and tell her.'

Before he appeared from behind the curtain, I knew. They both stepped into the room. As he sat down, his wife made a quick exit.

'Anna, the results are back.'

'Yes, I know.'

The doctor sat with a cup in his hand, his head bowed.

'I'm afraid the results aren't good. Your test is positive.'

And as I looked at this silver-haired man with his head bowed, it looked like he was going to cry, not me.

'I know,' I said. 'I had a feeling. I heard you and your wife talking. I've waited a month for you to tell me the results of that test, and that month has been one of the longest and hardest of my life. At least I know now.'

How could I be saying this so calmly to the doctor when another part of me wanted to run out of there as fast as my legs could carry me? It's hard to put words on how I felt. Looking back now, I realise there was no right or wrong way to respond to news like that. I was partly in shock, but I was also hearing something that had been in the back of my mind for a long time; something that I knew but didn't want to face. I know that there was a huge amount of fear, of confusion, going around in my head, trying to work out if I'd have to move back to Dublin; would I be able to live in the village or would I be even more isolated there when I got sick. All the other questions too, about my children, how I would tell my family. I had to give myself time to let it sink in.

'I've never had to tell someone this news before. You're my first patient. I'm very sorry.'

'It's OK. You see, I'm a survivor. But I just want you to promise me one thing, that you'll always be honest with me, no matter what.'

'In what way, Anna?'

'When it comes to tests or results or any illness that I may be facing, I need to know that you're going to be honest and tell it as it is.'

'Of course. Anything at all.'

'Because I'll need a good Doctor to get me through this.'

'I'm going to be honest right now and tell you I don't know an awful lot about HIV and AIDS. As I said, I've never treated anyone who's positive before.'

'Good. We can learn together so.'

After some more questions I thanked him and walked out the door. All I kept thinking about was how was I going to cope with this on my own? What would happen to my children? Would it be a big secret that I would have to carry around with me for the rest of my life, unable to talk about it for fear of being shunned? I couldn't come up with any answers.

Back home Deirdre was minding the children. When I arrived at my door I couldn't remember how I got there. Outside I took a deep breath of cold air. It was nearly Christmas.

She knew by my face what the results were. I could sense her fidgeting all around me in the kitchen, reluctant to say the words.

'Well, how did you get on?'

'I'm positive.'

'Jesus, Mary and Joseph.'

'I can't believe it,' I said to her as she put her arms out and hugged me with one of her motherly hugs. I started to sob great gulps of disbelief until I thought my breath would go from me. Deirdre just held me there as I cried and cried. Then I heard one of my children laugh in the other room. They had written their Santa letters and were now looking for socks to hang up. They were shouting in to me to help them find some.

'Mammy will be there in a minute,' Deirdre called to them before turning back to me. 'Anna, I'm going to take my kids up home to give you a bit of peace, but I'll be back down after a while and we can talk. You'll be OK until then, won't you?'

'Yeh. You go on ahead.'

After I had gathered the children up for bed, said our goodnights and given our kisses, I gazed into the open fire. On the mantelpiece hung four children's socks. All different colours and sizes. Some stuffed with more paper than others. This was my life. My children were my life and no virus was going to take that away.

I was putting more logs on the fire when a knock came to the window. It was Deirdre. 'Told you I wouldn't be long.'

'Do you want a cup of tea?'

'No. I brought something a bit stronger.' And out of her shopping bag she took a large bottle of whiskey.

That was Deirdre, a good friend. We poured ourselves a drink, sat and talked about my result. We laughed and cried into the early hours of the morning. I knew little or nothing, my doctor was a novice and Deirdre told me all she knew. It was she who gave me the helpline number of a support service in Galway called AIDS West. I didn't even know it existed. She told me it was completely confidential and to ring them if I had any questions. There were people out there to help me and support me through this.

Simon had become infected with HIV through using dirty needles and it was sexually transmitted from him to me. I had to accept my responsibility in this for not being careful. I had put myself at risk and now I had to live with the consequences of that. Living with HIV was not going to be easy, but I was certain while I had to live with it I wasn't going to allow it to take over my life. HIV would be part of it, but I was determined to carry on doing the normal regular stuff young mothers do. I had no choice but to function; my children depended on me. I'm sure it would have been easy for me to lie down under it all and wallow in it, but I'm not that type of person. I'm a fighter, a survivor.

A couple of days later I rang the number Deirdre had given me. A friendly voice answered. I didn't know what to say at first or even what to ask. I didn't know what it was I was supposed to know. I felt nervous and I felt stupid. The friendly voice was a woman called Emma and right from the start she put me at ease. She listened to my story and though she couldn't reverse my result, she made me see a little ray of hope that I wasn't able to see up to this. From that day on I knew I'd made an important connection with an organisation that would remain in my life and support me for many years to come.

My relationship with Dr. O'Brien was based on a solid foundation of trust. The fact that I was to be his first patient with HIV, I believe had its many advantages, if you can call them that. It was new to him and new to me too. He told me how he would read up on HIV and AIDS in his medical journals and went out of his way to find the latest information. We began exchanging literature and if either of us found a good book we'd recommend it. He looked forward to the quarterly newsletter from AIDS West and encouraged me to write articles for it. We learned about this infection of mine from each other. I didn't become a hypochondriac and he took a great interest in me as a person and as a patient. He was a wonderful support to me over the years and still is a great doctor and friend.

A strange incident took place that Christmas. I had a visit from the local shop owner.

'Hi, Anna. I just thought I'd drop this over. It's the TV you won.'

'I won a TV? No there must be a mistake. I didn't enter any competitions.'

'No, there's no mistake. You won it in the raffle.'

'But I didn't buy any raffle tickets.'

'Well, I don't know. Your number came out. Happy Christmas, Anna.'

Looking at him bewildered I replied, 'Happy Christmas to you, too.'

'Kids, we won a telly.'

My sister Sandra was the first in the family to hear my news. She relayed the information to the rest of them. Everyone was shocked. After the shock came the anger; anger at me for allowing it to happen; anger at Simon for passing the virus on to me. Echoes of 'that bastard, hope he rots in hell,' would often be heard when my family visited. They had taken the news of me being diagnosed HIV positive very badly. I found it hard to deal with their reaction, even though I could understand it. I needed time to get my head around it all before I could face their distress. That's when AIDS West was there for me. Having now met me, they arranged for a lovely woman in Galway city to become my befriender. A befriender is like a buddy or friend who offers emotional and sometimes practical support to someone who's HIV positive. A companion, a friendly voice at the end of a phone, and often a whole lot more. That person for me was Jean. She was my sanity when I had none, and my rock in a very hard place.

I'd been to see Dr. O'Brien again that January and he suggested that I should make an appointment with the doctor in the Galway hospital. He also said it would be a good idea to make a list of questions that I wanted him to answer for me. So I did as he suggested and set off for the hospital. The clinic was a cold place and not very uplifting. My first impressions of the doctor I have to admit weren't up to much, but armed with my questions I started. How would I know when I was seriously sick? How effective was the treatment and how would I know when to start it? I plodded along asking one by one until I got to my final question.

'What is the likelihood of me developing full-blown AIDS?'

'I'll put it to you this way. You're dying.' was his answer.

I was so shocked I didn't know what to say to him. I got up and walked out the hospital gates. All that went through my head was 'I'm dying. I'm dying.' This went through my head for days and at some time I must have rang Jean and told her the news. She was as shocked as I was. 'How does he know? Does he think he's the Almighty? How does he know he's not going to be dead before you?'

I laughed. Had we come nowhere in the past ten years since the virus hit the headlines. Had people learned nothing? However, Jean soon settled me down. She was always there to listen and offer sound advice.

My next encounter with the doctor wasn't any better, but this time I was ready for him. I was again in his clinic for a check-up, when he said, 'I think I need to refer you to our Social Work Department.'

'And what do I need to see a social worker for?'

'Because you're destitute and in need of help.'

'Destitute? Where are you getting "you're destitute" from? I'm by no means destitute. I'm a young mother with young children and I'm HIV positive. Not destitute. My name is Anna, Anna Mahon and I'm not just another number on your chart. Do you hear me? I'm not a number. My name is Anna and I'm not destitute, just HIV positive. OK.'

Taking off his glasses he stared at me. I could feel his eyes going through me. I didn't move.

I'm sorry Anna. You're right.'

'I just want you to see me as a person, not a number. Numbers don't have feelings.'

I needed him to see that I was still a person, that I wasn't the virus, nor was I ever going to be the virus. It was something in my life that I was going to have to live with, and there were so many more important things in it already, my children for one thing. I was not going to be labelled by anyone, no matter who they were.

From then on Mr. Doctor and I got on just fine.

Then one morning I woke up in terrible pain. I had a toothache, and the painkillers didn't work. I had to get to a dentist. Deirdre stepped in to mind the children while I got the bus to the city. I had the usual anaesthetic to numb the gum before the tooth was extracted. 'That's a relief now that it's gone,' I thought, as I hopped back on the bus home. The children were in from school when I arrived. They filled me in on their day.

'We had P.E. today.' Damien got in there first with his news. He was seven years old now and seemed to be getting taller by the day, with jet black hair and big brown eyes.

'And how's my Ray Ray?' I turned to look at Rachel sitting playing with her doll, her pigtails swinging.

'Can we go see the sheep at the weekend?'

'Yes of course we can.'

'Everything was fine here, Anna. Try to get some rest for yourself and don't be doing too much.'

'I won't. That's after knocking the stuffing out of me.'

Deirdre had only gone when I noticed the bleeding. 'It'll stop soon,' I told myself. Six hours later it still hadn't stopped and large clots were coming from the gaping hole in my gum. I was beginning to feel very weak. I called Dr. O'Brien. He came out and took one look at me.

'You're haemorrhaging. It's off to the hospital for you. You need a couple of stitches immediately.'

'Haemorrhaging? I can't go to the hospital now. I've no one to mind the kids. It'll have to wait 'til the morning.'

'No, you don't understand, Anna. You're haemorrhaging. If you don't get to the hospital tonight you'll be dead by then. Now, I'm ringing an ambulance.'

'Wait. No ambulance. I'll get Deirdre.'

Deirdre came as fast as she could and was at my doorstep with one of the local Gardaí. They always parked their cars near my house when they were on duty.

'Right Anna, come on. This nice garda here has offered to bring you into the hospital. Don't worry. I'll watch the kids.'

Where did I find this woman? She must have been sent from heaven to mind me, I thought as I was whisked away in the garda car covered in blood, sirens blaring.

Arriving at the A & E department of the hospital with a six foot, five inch garda and blood pouring out of me was a frightening experience for all those involved. Having to explain to the nursing staff in casualty that I was also HIV positive caused some panic because blood is one of the pathways to infection. They were very nervous around me. I was put on a trolley and brought in as an emergency. A dentist was woken from his bed and called to the hospital. I remember how shaky his hands were as he stitched me up. I was causing panic in him as well. They told me I had suffered a ruptured artery, haemorrhaged and lost four pints of blood. Nine stitches and several days later I was back home. Mam and Da had come down to mind the children. One of my brothers, who was a blood donor, offered to donate blood to me, but the doctor didn't want to give me a transfusion. He wanted my body to make up the loss itself, so I was weak for a long time. As I got a little stronger, I reassured my family that I was well again and they returned to Dublin. For a few days things looked good. Then one morning, I woke up freezing with the cold and couldn't get out of bed. I knew I was an emergency case. I told Damien to dress himself and Rachel, then to have a bit of breakfast, but to tell Deirdre that Mammy was sick when he met her at the school. Shortly after Deirdre arrived and called the doctor. She also rang Dublin again to tell them I'd took a bit of a turn. When Dr. O'Brien came he rang the ambulance. This time I didn't argue. It was pneumonia. As the ambulance men carried me out on the stretcher my dad arrived.

'Jesus. Is she going to be OK?'

'It's pneumonia,' the doctor said. 'She'll be in for a while.'

'Don't think she was right the first time they let her out after losing so much blood, Mr. Mahon,' Deirdre explained to my father, 'but she's in good hands now, they'll look after her.'

'Thanks, Deirdre. Don't know what we'd do without you.'

I was subjected to a lot of tests and given IV antibiotics to tackle the pneumonia. I was very weak. Reality was beginning to hit home. Is this what it was going to be like from now on? Was my immune system that weak? Would I recover?

CHAPTER 16

Slowly my energy began to return. It took nearly two months for me to get back on my feet, back to the home that meant so much to me.

I loved the village life, the peace and quiet, our walks to see the farm animals. I didn't miss Dublin at all and it was to be a year and a half later before I made my first visit back there. My return was not to see family or go a wild shopping trip, but for an appointment to see an HIV/AIDS specialist in Beaumont Hospital on Dublin's northside. I chose Beaumont as my treatment centre rather than St. James'. Both hospitals have top class HIV clinics, but there was a less likely chance of meeting someone I knew in Beaumont. You see the stigma HIV carried did affect me, even though I was doing my best not to let it.

The clinic for sexually transmitted infections was held once a week on the ground floor at the end of a maze of corridors. The leading consultant was a no-nonsense type of guy who was to be the doctor who helped me make medical decisions to do with my healthcare and treatment for many years to come. I knew right from the start that here I'd found myself what felt like another family. There was Julie, the social worker, all bubbly and full of energy. Yvonne, the really chilled-out secretary, who looked like she'd just stepped out of *Vogue* magazine. I often wondered why she hadn't pursued modeling, instead of being behind a desk taking appointments. But she loved her job and it did me good to see her friendly smile. And as for the nurses, they were second to none. The consultant had a wonderful team working with him and I was very glad to have them.

It was decided that there was no need for me to start on any treatment, and overall I was doing really well. My T-cells (CD4) count was around 900 and still within normal range. Measuring CD4 count is essential in monitoring the state of the immune system. The number of CD4 cells present is a direct indicator of the immune system's ability to fight off infections. The CD4 count of a person who is not infected with HIV may be anywhere between 500–1200. A count between 500–200 indicates that there has been some damage to the immune system and may be an indication of the need to start treatment. At 900, mine was still in good shape and I was learning more about HIV every day. Now with the team in Beaumont and the support of AIDS West in Galway I felt I could lead a normal and active life again. Having HIV wasn't the end of the world, but it was tough having a virus that you couldn't talk about. Cancer was a much more acceptable illness. HIV was certainly not in those days, and even today in many areas it still is not acceptable. Some believed (and still do) that it was God's way of punishing undesirables for the immorality of their ways. I knew HIV was something I was going to have to accept in my life and learn to take responsibility for my part in contracting it. This acceptance was something I felt only time would bring me. Yes, the virus was in my body, in my life, but I wasn't about to roll over and let it win.

Gareth had been sick a lot lately. His temperature soared and he suffered from diarrhoea. I was worried about him especially. I convinced myself my other three children were all negative and I had nothing to worry about with them, but with Gareth it was different. I'd blame myself for every cough or sneeze he had and constantly I'd walk the floor with him giving him Dioralite to try to settle his stomach. He was such a good baby, always smiling, except when he was sick which was starting to become more and more frequent. Inside my heart was breaking. Please God, don't let my baby be positive.

So I took the next leap – to have the children tested. Damien. Negative. Rachel. Negative. Alan. Negative. But when it came for Gareth to be tested, I couldn't do it.

Once again I buried my head in the sand. I got angry. I prayed for HIV to leave my life and I cursed Simon for ever coming into it. Having HIV is one thing, but knowing you could have passed it onto your baby is something totally different.

Then Gareth had his first seizure when he was nine months old and I ran out of the house screaming. I had never witnessed anyone having a seizure before and I was helpless. Thankfully my neighbour, Mary, heard my screams and came running.

'Anna, what is it?'

'It's the baby. I don't know what to do.'

Thankfully, she did. She took every stitch of clothes off him and put him in the sink to cool him down. When the doctor came he told me it was due to his temperature running too high. Febrile convulsions, he called it. Mary had nine children herself and one of them also took seizures. I thank God she was on hand for me that day. After that, alarm bells started going off in my head. Still I did nothing.

It wasn't until Gareth developed pneumonia some months later that I walked into the paediatrics department of the hospital and signed the consent form to have him tested for HIV. Gareth was now fifteen months old. The results were to be returned to Dr. O'Brien. Two weeks of hell followed. I spent the days praying and the nights crying myself to sleep. Whatever about me being positive, the idea of my baby having the virus and me being responsible was too much to bear. This was one result I couldn't hear on my own. I knew I just didn't have the strength to face it alone, so the day of the results I asked my mother to come with me to the surgery.

'Mam, I'm absolutely terrified. I'll never be able to live with myself if this test comes back positive.'

'You have to stop thinking the worst. We're here now. I've prayed so much for this day. Please God and the Blessed Mother he'll be fine.'

The receptionist called my name.

'Mam, come in with me, will you?' And as I rose to go in I felt every nerve in my body was gone. I was numb. The door opened.

'Hello, Anna. The test was negative. Gareth is negative. He doesn't have it.'

I fell into the chair, tears of joy running down my face.

'That's wonderful news, doctor.'

It was my mother talking. I was speechless.

'Yes it is. In fact it's more than that. It's a miracle.'

'Anna, it's a miracle. Did you hear that? I have prayed so hard for this day. It's all over now, Anna. It's a miracle.'

'Babies are different you see; it's likely Gareth was born with it, but has developed his own immune system now. Babies develop their own antibodies between 12–18 months. It really is a miracle.'

I'd never been happier in my life than that day and I thank God, the blessed mother and all the angels and saints in Heaven for my miracle.

In the spring of 1993 I moved house. A big part of me was sorry to leave the little village and the people who had opened their hearts and their homes to me and adopted me as one of their own. I reassured myself I wasn't going far, and told friends I'd be back to visit. After all I was only moving to a council house in the next town eight miles away.

It was a new house with a small front and back garden. It had three bedrooms, a bathroom, sitting room and kitchen. The kitchen had a range that you could also cook on. This was very complicated for a young Dublin woman who had never seen one before. It was a lovely house and as I looked out the bedroom window at the houses and fields that surrounded me, I told myself I was home and I was never moving again.

Little by little I built the home around the children, a home I'd always dreamed of, finding gardening and DIY skills I never thought I'd had. I made friends with the neighbours and settled the children into the local national school. I became more involved with AIDS West and the work they do. I began doing interviews for local radio and newspapers and giving talks to community groups, schools and colleges to raise awareness of HIV/AIDS. It was time for me to take a stand, to let people know that AIDS didn't just happen in Africa, people in Ireland got it too.

It was during this time I was in hospital having treatment for yet again another infection that a member of the Community Care Group came to visit me. All flustered, her name was Sr. Maura.

'Anna, you're going to have to move.'

'What are you talking about?'

'A certain somebody has been asking questions from your doctor about you and the children, and I think it's best if you move.'

'First of all, I'm not moving for anyone. Now what's this person's name and what exactly has she been saying?'

'You don't know her, Dr. O'Brien is away and she went into the locum doctor and made up this story that you had asked her to mind your children. She asked her what would happen if her kids bit your kids.'

'What? That's crazy. Who is this person?'

'Just some busybody.'

'And what did the locum say to this?'

'She told her she'd nothing to worry about; that your children are OK.'

'Right that's it; hand me over those clothes. I'm out of here. I need to sort this out and I can't do it from a hospital bed.'

'Anna. There's more. She's gone to the Parents' Council and the school wants to know where it stands regarding insurance for your children.'

Discharging myself from the hospital, I arrived home to be met by my mother at my door. She could see I was angry.

'What on earth are you doing home? You're not supposed to be back until Friday.'

I was like a woman possessed. Quickly I explained the story to her. I had no idea who this woman was. She probably heard me on one of the local interviews, put two and two together and was trying to get more information about me. But she didn't realise who she was dealing with; a lioness protecting her cubs.

I knew exactly what I had to do. Around I went to the doctor's surgery. I waited and waited to be called, and in I went.

'You don't know me. My name is Anna Mahon. I'm one of Dr. O'Brien's patients. And your name is?'

'Dr. Harper. I'm standing in for Dr. O'Brien while he's away.'

'I understand there was a woman making enquiries about me. Would you like to tell me exactly what was said?'

'Oh. Yes. Yes.' Searching for words she continued. 'She called today and told me she'd been asked to mind your children and was just wondering what would she do if her child was to bite one of yours. I told her she didn't have to worry about that. They were OK.'

'How dare you. First of all I don't know who she is. Nor have I ever asked anyone to mind my children. My mother minds my children when I'm sick. And another thing, I don't know you either. You're not my doctor.

Does that mean any Joe Soap can walk in off the street and ask you questions about me and my children?'

'No. Look, I'm really sorry about all this.'

'Sorry. You don't know what you've just done. Did you know that this person has gone to the Parents' Council and now the school wants to know where it stands regarding insurance?'

'No, I didn't. I'm really sorry. Is there anything I can do?'

'I think you've done enough already. Did you not swear a Hippocratic Oath when you became a doctor? Because I'm telling you this much, the next time you open your mouth about me or my children again, I'll have your job and your head. And another thing, just wait until I tell Dr. O'Brien what you've done.'

I stormed out of the surgery. The school did make enquiries through Sr. Maura. I informed Sr. Maura if the school had any concerns regarding this matter to contact Dr. O'Brien and he would confirm to them that my children were healthy and happy, despite the troublemakers of this world.

It was shortly after that incident occurred that I decided it was time for me to tell my two eldest children. I'd thought about it long and hard, and figured it was best they heard it from me rather than a nasty comment in the schoolyard. Damien was nine years old and Rachel was seven.

It was one fine summer's evening with the two younger children tucked up in their beds that I sat them down at the kitchen table to tell them about their mother's illness. I had bought a bag of green grapes as a special treat. Grapes were expensive. We didn't have them very often.

'How's school?'

Damien sat there bobbing his legs up and down, shooting pips into the bowl.

'Teacher's OK.'

'And you Rachel?'

'I've made new friends. Marie and Valerie.'

'I'm glad, because you see I want to tell you something. You know the way Mammy has to go to the hospital sometimes when she isn't well?'

They both nodded.

'But then you're better when you come home,' Damien said.

'Yes, that's right. Well, I wanted to tell you in case someone at school says something nasty to you about me. You see Mammy has a little cold in her blood. It's a virus called HIV and that's why she gets sick, and all around the world doctors are looking for a cure for people like me so that the little cold goes away.'

They said nothing to this, Damien was still plucking grapes from the bowl when Rachel jumped off the chair and went to the fridge. My eyes followed her. Opening the fridge she took out a bottle of her cough medicine and holding it in her hand, she proudly announced, 'soon a doctor somewhere in the world is going to find a cure for your cold. Because years ago we didn't have medicine for our coughs and now we do. So don't worry, Mammy.'

I had no answer to that. Hugging and kissing them, we all sat at the table munching our grapes. I talked to them about prejudice and discrimination and what it meant about different races and cultures. Big words for little children and I was surprised how much they knew, how much they understood. We talked about how black people weren't allowed on buses once and when they finally were, how they had to sit separately from white people for a long time until a woman named Rosa Parks stood up for herself and changed the law. I said how you didn't have to have different coloured skin for people to discriminate against you; that fear had an awful lot to do with peoples' prejudices. We talked some more about what it was like to be different and what it meant to keep an open mind and not judge people. We sat there, me telling them with grapes until their little eyes began to droop and there was nothing left but a bare stalk in the fruit bowl. Love and hope filled the room that night. The children learned so much, but then so did I.

CHAPTER 17

I always knew I wouldn't have far to look to find Simon. I had come to the stage where I didn't want to hide away anymore. I had spent so many days looking over my shoulder, terrified he was behind me; I could no longer go on like that. I was ready to confront my fears and lay ghosts to rest. I'd been gone four years and I needed to move on from that. I wanted to show him how I had moved on, how I had built up my life despite what went before. I heard he hadn't been seen around the streets of Dublin for a while, so I knew I wouldn't have far to look for him. The Big Hotel. I rang Mountjoy Prison and asked if he was there. He was and I requested a visit. It was granted to me.

As I sat in the bus, whizzing past fields of sheep or horses, stone walls, towns busy about their business, my stomach was sick with nerves. As we passed through Athlone, Kilbeggan, Kilcock, I knew I just had to do this. I wondered how he would look after all this time; would he be stoned? I had to see him face to face to put closure on that part of my life. Soon I found myself outside the gates of Mountjoy Prison with a visiting slip in my hand. I didn't know what he was in for this time, and I wasn't going to ask. But I knew I could only do this while he was in a restrained environment. I could never have done it if we met on the street. Behind bars he couldn't touch me. Half of me wanted to tell him how well I was doing and how much I'd moved on with my life, and the other half wanted to curse him and tell him how much he'd destroyed it. So it was with very mixed feelings that I searched for his face amongst the other prisoners. Then I spotted him in the last room, sitting in the middle row, fidgeting with his hands. I could see he was as nervous as I was. I looked into his eyes before I sat down. He wasn't stoned.

'How ya, Anna? What has you up here?'

'Maybe to ask you some things.'

Any love I had for him was well buried as I sat before him.

'It's great to see ya. I've waited a long time for this day to come. Tell me how's the kids? Everything's OK with them, is it?'

'Yeh. They're fine.'

'They must be big now. Did you bring any photos up with ya?'

'No, I didn't.'

He was upset by this. I was upset by the fact that he knew I was pregnant when I left, but he didn't ask about another child.

'So what's this all about, Anna? If you want me to get back with ya, you can forget that. I'm going out with someone else now. I was expecting her up today but I took your visit instead.'

'No, I'm just here to ask you why you did all those horrible things to me?'

'Jaysus sake, Anna. You know it was the drugs. When you're on the gear ya don't care about anyone or anything. All ya care about is getting the next hit.'

'It's so easy for you to blame the drugs. Always blaming someone or something else, it's never just you. I can't believe you could think I'd come up and want you back. I wouldn't want you back if you were the last man on earth, after all the pain you caused me.'

'Look, I'm sorry. Is that what you want to hear?'

His apology meant nothing.

'Well, what do ya want then? Do you want me to nail meself to the wall to show ya how sorry I am? Ya know I'll always love ya. You're the mother of me kids, for God's sake.'

'I didn't come to listen to this.'

'Anna, look me head's cabbaged.'

'What? Your head is like a cabbage?'

'No, ya dope.' Laughter brightened his face. 'I said me head's cabbaged.'

'I don't know what that means.'

'It means for someone so intelligent, you're so stupid.'

'I have to go.'

'Anna, give us a kiss.' He leaned forward on the dividing table. I looked at him and froze.

'No way.'

'That's OK then.'

He stretched out his hand.

I shook it.

'Take care of yourself and the kids.'

'Goodbye, Simon.'

And that was it. I'd done what I'd come to do.

CHAPTER 18

A friend of mine in Galway invited me to her art exhibition one evening. She told me to bring along a couple of friends, to enjoy the free wine and the craic. I have to admit I was never the arty, farty type but I went along to show support and took Marie and Sue with me for company. As it turned out it was a wonderful evening. I admired the paintings and enjoyed the wine. I had great fun watching my friend Sue stuttering and blubbering, as Liam Ó Maonlaí from the Hothouse Flowers entered the room to open the exhibition. If ever I saw someone fall head over heels it was Sue that night, but Liam being the modest gentleman that he was couldn't see what the fuss was about. Sue and Marie being his newfound groupies, I decided to remain in the background, quietly giggling.

After the exhibition we were on a roll and as the laughter continued we said we'd hit a club and make a night of it. So when this fine young man asked me if I'd like a dance I thought all my birthdays had come together. He told me his name was Marty. He was 25, from Dublin and was now working in Galway. He seemed really nice. We had a couple of dances together and I returned to my friends. 'Me and relationships don't work,' I told myself. As we were leaving the club to get a taxi home, I heard someone call my name. Halfway down the street I could see Marty.

'Right girls, run.'

'You crazy woman. What are you doing?' Sue said.

'Come on, I don't want to talk to him.'

And as we ran through the streets of Galway laughing and giggling, dodging the people and the traffic, I felt I was sixteen again. Just as I was about to get into the taxi, Marty tapped me on the shoulder. He was out of breath. There were rip-roaring cheers from inside the taxi.

'Anna, I'd like to see you again. Can I give you a ring?'

Silence in the taxi.

'Well, if you're willing to run through the streets of Galway after me ...'

He wrote my number on the back of his hand.

'Hooray, Hooray,' came the cheers from the two lunatics sitting inside.

'I'll call you tomorrow.'

And he did. We arranged to go to see a film that next weekend. I was so nervous. My first date in God knows how long. I must have changed my clothes at least five times. Just as I was ready to leave, the heavens opened, but it didn't dampen my spirits and we spent a lovely evening together. Marty was a very funny, young man; I forgot all my worries and laughed the night away. But when it was time to go home I was reluctant to make another date. I just said I'd stay in touch.

I could never again see myself in a relationship with another man. I told him I had four children. He was a bit shocked at first, yet it didn't put him off. I could tell him that, but I couldn't tell him my secret. I mean, how can you tell someone you've just met that you're HIV positive? So I refused to see him and buried my feelings. His phone calls continued.

Late November, I was admitted to hospital with a respiratory infection; put on IV antibiotics and fluids. I knew World AIDS Day was coming up on December the first, so I asked the staff if I could get out for a couple of hours for the candlelit memorial service in Eyre Square arranged by AIDS West. Here people placed red ribbons on the huge Christmas tree as a gesture of support for people living with HIV and in memory of those who had died. The hospital agreed. I also arranged to meet Marty there. At first he was a bit bewildered as to why I wanted to meet him at a Christmas tree, so I told him about the candlelight service and what it meant. He understood. He also understood when later I told him I had to go back to the hospital. I was one of those people who were being supported by AIDS West. I was someone living with HIV.

There is no easy way of telling someone that news because you never know how a person is going to react. Having friends and forming new relationships was now going to be difficult for me. Socially, mentally and physically, HIV was going to affect my life and bring with it lots of changes.

Yet, that December night as I stood holding hands with Marty and the children's choir sang *Little Drummer Boy* around the tree, I knew my life was about to change.

'I still want to be part of your life, Anna,' he whispered, as he wrapped his arms around me.

My mother couldn't understand at first why I'd bother with any man. Sure wasn't I better off on my own? But once she met Marty and got to know him a little bit, I think she saw in him what I did … a good heart. And as for the children, once they learned he worked in a toyshop he got their vote too. Marty and I became an item and the children gave him a nickname 'Martypops.' We went everywhere together.

CHAPTER 19

A peer support group for HIV positive people was set up in Galway by AIDS West. There were five in that original group, Emer, Paul, Franco, Hans and me. We all hit it off pretty well. Emer and I became good friends. The first night we met, she drove me home in her van. We talked a lot about HIV and how it affected our lives. She was the first woman I had met who was HIV positive and willing to talk about it. I often felt we had a lot in common even though we had lived different lives, hers in different countries and mine running up and down the length and breath of my own. I often visited Emer at home. We'd sit and listen to music and have a coffee. I loved hearing her tales of travelling the world and I'd dream of sitting on a sun-kissed beach in some far-off land, sipping cocktails. Motorbikes were another of her passions. I admired her independence, her strength and her love of life. Often we'd visit each other in hospital or she'd sing another Queen classic *The Show Must Go On* down the phone if I was feeling low.

I was surprised when I got a phone call to say she had been admitted to hospital in Dublin. She had been on a train to Dublin to go to see the Aerosmith concert when she developed pains in her hands and feet. She didn't make it to the concert, but ended up in St. James' instead. I went to visit her there and was upset to see how unwell she had become. She had also started AZT treatment but what shocked me most was that she was unable to walk. The doctor diagnosed peripheral neuropathy. HIV was attacking her nervous system. Emer came out of hospital in a wheelchair and never walked again. She suffered from fatigue and malaise. She lost her appetite, had regular bouts of respiratory infections and later developed P.C.P., Pneumocystis carinii pneumonia, one of the many opportunistic infections that affect people who are HIV and have a low CD4 count.

Opportunistic infections as their name implies, occur when the immune system of someone who is HIV positive is so compromised that bacteria, viruses or parasites seize the opportunity to attack the body and infect it. P.C.P. is a common parasite that is found throughout the world. Generally it is not a problem in a healthy immune system. The majority of people are infected in childhood where it remains dormant unless the immune system has been weakened in any way. It attacks the lungs and is an infection that was rare prior to the arrival of HIV. This is what Emer's body was trying to cope with, but was too weak to overcome. It came as an awful blow when I heard she had died.

We were both in the hospital at the same time, but I was too sick to visit her, and when I got out, Jean was at the doorstep to tell me the sad news. I went to the funeral but it all went by in a blur. She was only thirty three. I can still remember the funny laugh she used to have and when I smell lavender to this day I think of her. She used the herb to relax her when she felt overstressed.

Emer was the first close friend I had that I lost because of this virus, but she wasn't the last. Franco and Hans also both died shortly after that. Hans often visited me when I was in hospital; he was in his late twenties, a fine, handsome man. The first time he came to visit me, he brought me a big red apple wrapped in tissue paper. It wasn't long after Emer's death that Hans too began to go downhill. His appetite went out the window and the weight fell off him. HIV advanced and despite the treatments that were available at the time, Han's immune system became weaker. He too developed opportunistic infections; one of them was called C.M.V., Cytomegalovirus. C.M.V. is a common virus that is usually harmless and rarely causes illness. A healthy immune system can hold the virus in check. But if it is seriously compromised by something like HIV, the virus is activated and causes C.M.V. It infects the entire body and towards the end of his life, Hans lost the vision in one of his eyes and had only partial vision in the other. He developed fever, fatigue and had difficulty breathing. All too soon I was saying goodbye to another friend. Franco died soon after that when his immune system also gave up. I was going to funerals of people who had the same virus as I had and that was very scary. I felt even more isolated. I had made real friendships with people in circumstances similar to myself, people who helped me and made me see the good things in life and now they were dead. I was alone again.

In the months that followed Emer's death, I asked her family for their permission to make a panel for the Irish AIDS Memorial Quilt in her memory. They gave their approval and Emer's sister lovingly made and added her contributions too. Each was a symbol of her life and a token of our love for her.

The idea of an AIDS Memorial Quilt was conceived in November 1985 in San Francisco by gay rights activist Cleve Jones. Jones was involved in planning an annual candlelit march, honouring gay San Francisco Supervisor Harvey Milk and Mayor George Moscone who had been assassinated in 1978. While organising the march, he discovered that over one thousand San Franciscans had died from AIDS. He asked each of the marchers to write on placards the names of friends and family who had died from the virus. These were then taped to the walls of the San Francisco Federal Building when the march was over. This huge display of names resembled a patchwork quilt. Jones was so taken by this sight he was inspired to create a larger memorial. The following year he created the first panel of what was to become the AIDS Memorial Quilt in memory of one of his friends, Marvin Feldman. In June of 1987, he and a number of others gathered together to document the lives of those who had died from AIDS and thereby help people understand the devastating impact of the disease, thus establishing the foundation of the NAMES Project, the AIDS Memorial Quilt.

When a display of thousands of assembled panels was erected on the National Mall in Washington D.C. during the national march on Washington for Lesbian and Gay Rights in October that year, it caught the public imagination and established the Quilt as America's National AIDS Memorial. It covered a space larger than a football field and five hundred thousand people came to see it that weekend. The response led to a four-month national tour that gathered momentum as it went from state to state. Local panels were added at each venue, tripling its size by the end of the tour. By 1992 the Quilt included panels from every state as well as twenty-eight other countries.

To date over forty-four-thousand individual panels have been made. Each panel measures three feet by six feet – the size of a standard grave – and usually carries the person's name and details of their life, their work, interests or hobbies, along with messages of love from its creators. The panels are richly decorated, often with striking colours and images, so that when displayed they are not only emotionally but also visually stunning. Worldwide, the Quilt has been established as a powerful symbol of remembrance for those who have died, and of hope for those living with AIDS. Ireland soon became part of the biggest community art project and Emer's Quilt panel was the first named panel in the West of Ireland. It has joined the Irish Quilt tour and has been displayed not only in Ireland but also overseas. I'm sure she would have been proud of our achievement.

When one of the neighbours around the corner refused to let my daughter Rachel play with her child because 'there's bad blood in that family,' I knew it was time to take more steps to rid society of the ignorance and prejudice that surrounded me, and there was no better place to start than in the town that I now called home. I refused to be 'witch-hunted' and I wasn't going to sit back and watch my children being shunned.

In November 1996 after months of planning, I organised an AIDS Awareness Weekend. I got some local bands together. A boy dance group travelled from Dublin and donations of spot prizes from the local shops poured in for the raffle. The Irish AIDS Memorial Quilt was brought down from Dublin and displayed in the secondary school. I told the story of the Quilt to anyone who would listen. And everyone did. From first years to sixth years, they all sat in silence. I knew I had captured their attention, and when the school children went home they told their parents the story of the Quilt, educating the family as a whole about HIV. When the Parents' Council asked if I would kindly do a special display for them and tell them the story too, I knew I'd cracked it. However we ran into trouble when the local priest refused to mention the event because it was an issue that didn't concern the parish. Now that I had people on my side there was uproar. He was inundated with phone calls from irate parents asking 'what do you mean it doesn't concern the parish? HIV/AIDS affects everyone and we want to know about it.' Needless to say he wasn't long changing his mind. Neither was the mother who turned up her nose at me when I was selling tickets for the AIDS West Benefit Gig that I'd arranged. As she slammed the door in my face, I heard her teenage daughter scream at her and the mother came running down the garden after me, apologising and asking if she could buy not one but four tickets to the Gig.

The Benefit Gig was a huge success. The local bands played everything from Van Morrison to Led Zeppelin. They even played Queen's *The Show Must Go On*. The dance group from Dublin was a big hit with the teenage girls and many a tear was shed as they waved goodbye to their idols at the train station. Somewhere up there Emer was smiling. I'd done it. I'd accomplished what I had set out to do. The Irish AIDS Awareness weekend had changed people's attitudes and the Irish AIDS Memorial Quilt had touched everyone's heart.

CHAPTER 20

I'd never had a passport nor travelled any further than Holyhead when I was seven and my sister had told me the boat was sinking. I was terrified I was going to drown and didn't want to get on a boat for a long time. However, as I got older I had great ambitions to become a social worker and to travel the world. Then I met Simon and all my dreams went out the window.

But now I was almost thirty, Simon wasn't in my life and I was getting my first passport. Sr. Maura had arranged a trip to Lourdes for my mother and me. The trip came so unexpectedly that it was almost too late for me to get one. My brother-in-law had to collect it from the passport office the day before we were due to fly out and then to drive down to Galway with it. It felt official now as I stood in the kitchen holding that all important document. I was going places. The excitement of it all nearly gave my poor mother a heart attack when she heard she was going. She had always dreamed of going there, but could never see how it might happen, and now here she was busily packing her best clothes, shoes, sun hats and cream and everything but the kitchen sink into the suitcase she had bought for the occasion. Neither of us got a wink of sleep the night before. Martypops had offered to mind the children and I knew they would be in safe hands.

The day of our departure finally arrived and off we headed to Shannon Airport. We travelled with a group from Galway. They were a mixture of people with various illnesses and disabilities, carers, a great priest who entertained us throughout the trip with his music and his songs and, of course, the bishop. My mother was delightfully embarrassed as she posed for a photograph with him. The photo turned out well and I know it was something she treasured for the rest of her life. A proud moment captured. Another memorable moment was when she had her photo taken as she boarded the plane with her duty-free bag containing her valuables (her cigarettes). I could see she was already in Heaven. She didn't need to go to Lourdes.

My first impression of Lourdes was that it was like walking into another world. I was mesmerised by the number of people from Ireland, from all over the world who had come to this place of pilgrimage, of miracles; all gathered to be healed in some way. It gave out a great feeling of calm and peace. We took it all in: the visit to the Grotto, the freezing cold baths (and the miracle of being bone dry when you stepped out) and the candlelit processions. I loved to watch the ribbon of lights as people carried them in the dark on the nightly vigil to the Grotto, different flags and banners being carried by representatives from parishes all over Ireland. The candlelit procession is something I believe would touch even the non-believer. It's an awesome experience to watch thousands of people holding candles and singing the *Ave Maria*. It was all deeply moving.

The other side of the coin was the rows and rows of stalls selling beads and pictures of the Grotto in all shapes and sizes, plastic toys and little bottles of holy water – everyone trying to cash in on the miracle. But I loved that part of it too, walking along the streets in the heat, watching all the people as they bought their souvenirs. Then, just before we were scheduled to fly home, I got sick with a respiratory infection and was sent to the infirmary. The doctors discussed as to whether it was safe for me to fly home. My mother said she'd never heard of anyone going to Lourdes and getting sick. Finally they consented and I was allowed return home.

'It could only happen to you,' she said. 'Most people get cured here.'

Once back from Lourdes I got the bug – the travel bug that is. I couldn't wait to go away again. But travelling cost money and I didn't have much of that lying around. So I decided to get myself a job. That job was working on a community employment scheme as a housing support worker with the Simon Community. The work involved looking after long-term homeless men in residential settings, helping them help themselves, shopping, cooking and social trips. And I loved it. The work was sometimes challenging for me, often rewarding and always great craic. We had many social outings, barbeques, Christmas parties, a trip to the zoo and the beach. I was meeting new people and for the first time in a long while I felt like I belonged somewhere. I was feeling well most of the time and my illness seemed to be under control. Marty and I had a holiday on the Greek island of Corfu. I told him if I started to talk to the wall to get worried as I might do a Shirley Valentine. Corfu is a beautiful island, but I don't think anything could have prepared me for the intense heat or the mosquitoes, for that matter. No amount of repellent would stave them off such was their love of me.

We went on two boat trips, one to the tiny island of Paxos and the other to Albania. Albania was a beautiful country, the little I saw of it, but somehow it seemed to be caught in a time warp; the few cars we saw were vintage and shops had little or nothing to sell. The economy was in troubled times. Our tour guide told us that it would take a month's wages to buy a pair of shoes. Somehow the meal arranged for our group at a four star hotel consumed me with guilt, when all around me there were little children begging for food. Also two weeks away from my own children was far too long and by the end of the holiday, I was totally homesick. Never again would I go away for so long without them. So the following year, we took the children away for their first holiday to Spain. It was such a different look at life for them, they could barely sit for a meal they were so excited to see everything, do everything. Jumping in and out of the pool, playing pool, running into the sea in the dark. A holiday they still talk about to this day and will remember for the rest of their lives. Life was good.

Then I got a phone call from my sister in Dublin one day, asking if I'd bought one of the Sunday papers.

'Why?' I asked her.

'Because your dearly beloved is all over it.'

And she was right. Mr. Crime's story was there for all to see, including a photo of him being led away to prison. As I turned the pages I couldn't believe what I was reading. It was his story of how he got involved in drugs and crime. That part made me feel sad, but when I got to the part where he said his wife had left him with the three kids, I was livid. How dare he mention me or the children. How easy it was for him to put his own spin on the story. Reading on, it said, despite his involvement with drugs, he was negative to the virus that causes AIDS. Who did he think he was kidding? Anyone reading it could tell he was rejoicing in his own glory. 'So where does that leave me?' I thought. 'That's it. I'm going up to Mountjoy Prison and I'm going to kill him.'

I applied for visiting rights and in the queue with a visiting slip, I once again found myself at the gates of Mountjoy Prison. I was going to give him a piece of my mind. Walking into the visiting room, Simon sat with his head bowed.

'How are ya, Anna?'

'Don't you how ya me.'

'Jaysus, you didn't come up to argue, did ya?'

'What do you think you're playing at? Splashed all over the Sunday papers?'

'Look, it was just some fool writing about me.'

'You should be ashamed of yourself. Have you no bloody shame at all. Bringing me and the kids into your life of crime. And what's this about you being HIV negative?'

'Yeh. That's right, I'm grand. I had another test and it was negative.'

'That's a load of crap and you know it.'

'Anyway, how's the kids? They must be big now. Would you not bring them up on a visit Anna?'

'You have to be joking.'

'It just would be nice to see them, that's all.'

'You chose your life of drugs and crime, not me.'

'But Anna, I still love ya. You're in my blood and I'm in yours.'

His words floored me. I sat and stared at him. His blood in mine. If only he knew that what he was saying was really true in more ways than one. But I wasn't about to tell him.

'I've moved on with my life, Simon, and me and the children are very happy. I don't need to be picking up the Sunday newspaper to read about you blowing your own trumpet. Next time you do it, leave me and the children out of it.'

'There won't be a next time. I'm sorry.'

As I looked to leave, I saw for the first time the broken man he'd become. His life of drugs and crime had taken their toll. The scars on his face and hands had aged him more than his years.

CHAPTER 21

All I remember was Jean driving me to the hospital in Galway. I had been feeling unwell for a while now, hoping to shake off the bug I had, but without success. I was stretched out on the back seat of her car going in and out of a deep sleep, finding it hard to breathe. I was admitted to an isolation unit. Doctors suspected it was P.C.P. or pneumocystis carinii pneumonia which is an opportunistic infection. This was the infection that Emer had died from five years earlier, and if I wasn't so sick I'd have been very, very scared. They treated me with a number of drugs, including Septrin to try and get the pneumonia under control, but it didn't seem to be having any affect. I remember feeling really cold and turning blue. When the nurse took my temperature, it was 105°F. There was a fan in the room but it wasn't enough and I had to crawl out of bed to the sink and stick my head under the cold running water to try and cool down. The medication made me feel really sick; I seemed to be getting worse instead of better. I was sure I wasn't that sick when I came in. Days went by in a haze of fever though I do remember the ward sister coming into my room at one point and asking me.

'What's this, Anna?' as she held up the tray.

'It's my cup, my plate, my spoon, my knife and fork,' I mumbled, too weak to fight anymore. The hospital isolated the dishes I used because of their fear of HIV. They were still working on the mistaken belief that it could be transmitted through crockery. I was too ill to be giving the hospital staff a lecture on the routes of infection of HIV or to fight their prejudice. I needed someone else to do that for me.

'I'll see about this,' she continued. 'I used to work as a nurse in San Francisco and this sort of discrimination wouldn't have been tolerated and I won't accept this ignorant behaviour here either.'

She took the tray and stormed out. Whatever she said or did it worked because for all my meal-times after that, I no longer had to use my own utensils or crockery. But I was disturbed another day when two large men came into my room and moved my bed, with me in it, out to the corridor in order to scrub the floor. Along came the ward sister.

'What's the meaning of this? Why is that woman being put out on the corridor?'

'We were told to clean the room.'

'Get out, the pair of you and bring that bed back in there.'

And that was the end of that.

I stopped the Septrin because I was vomiting too much. The doctor said it would be on my own head if I discontinued the medication. But I didn't care. I pulled the drips out and told them all to leave me alone. I'd get better myself. And I did. Two weeks later I was allowed home. There were valuable lessons learned. Ignorance and prejudice were alive and well in the hospital, though thankfully amongst only a minority of staff. How long would it take before people would let go of the stigma around the disease? As we neared the 21st century, I really hoped it would come someday. Another lesson learned was that I was allergic to Septrin, one of the main drugs used to treat P.C.P.

I was aware of how sick I'd been, how close I came to maybe not making it, and I promised myself I wouldn't leave it so long before I sought medical help in the future. Day by day I got stronger and was soon back on my feet again. Shortly after that I gave a public talk in the Great Southern Hotel in Galway as part of an AIDS Awareness Education night. So many people turned up to hear me talk they had to open the ballroom to accommodate them.

In front of over two hundred people I spoke about my life and what it was like living with HIV, the stigma attached to the virus and how it affected me and my children. To my surprise, I got a standing ovation and afterwards, six student nurses from the hospital came up and thanked me for giving a wonderful talk. They told me they never thought of what it must be like for those affected by HIV and promised that in their future careers as nurses, wherever in the world it brought them, they would now have more understanding of HIV/AIDS.

Some years later I was to encounter one of those student nurses who had been in the group that night. Now qualified, she sat by my bedside and told me she remembered me and the talk I gave and how much it had changed her life. She told me that before she met me that night she had been thinking of giving up nursing, but listening to me had made her change her mind and stay with it.

CHAPTER 22

Everyone was talking about the millennium; the festivities they had planned for their New Year's bash that would bring them into the 21st century. Each household in Ireland received a millennium candle as a memento of this special occasion. Nostradamus prophecies made world-wide headlines. Was this really the end? Would computers all over the world crash down and cause chaos because of the super powers of the millennium bug? Who would be the millennium baby? Would we have electricity in the morning? Ireland and the world went mad. It was the turn of the century and a time for new beginnings.

Marty had moved back to Dublin in the summer of 1999. He felt Dublin held more job opportunities for him. He had left the toy store behind and had been working with a security firm for a number of years now. Doing security meant he worked nights and I worked days. We weren't seeing a lot of one another. He was fed up stuck in dead-end jobs and felt his life was going nowhere. So a return to Dublin for him had always been on the cards. I missed him very much when he left. I knew the children adored him and he was a good man. Often they'd ask, 'When's Martypop coming down?' To them he was always great fun; always coming up with new places to go, things to do and new adventures.

Like the time he took us on an Easter egg treasure hunt to Ailwee Caves, Co. Clare. He made sure that we set off early to be there first. Sitting on a hill with over a hundred cars behind us, the handbrake went and Marty's car went sliding. An explosion of laughter came from everyone in the back seat as he tried to manoeuvre the car up the hill using the footbrake to prevent him crashing into anyone. It rained heavily that day but it didn't stop us in our treasure hunt for Cadbury's Creme Eggs. We were all sick from chocolate on the way home. Or the time we went to

Butlin's, Co. Meath and I dressed up the two youngest for the fancy-dress competition. Alan was John Wayne with a carton of milk in his hand and a sign around his neck that said, *Get off your horse and drink some milk.* I dressed Gareth in toilet roll from head to toe with a sign that read, *Andrexis the Mummy.* Yes, we had lots of happy times, and along with that came stability during the years he was with us.

Marty came down to celebrate the millennium with us. My sister, her husband and their youngest child also came and spent that time with us. Holding hands, we sang *Auld Lang Syne* and together we partied until the small hours of the morning.

That millennium night was to be a turning point for me. Marty wanted us to come back and live in Dublin. It was something we had talked about, but I dismissed. We were happy in the country, the children were settled there, and I managed very well unless I got sick. Moving back to Dublin had always, it seemed, been out of the question for me. Marty and I had come to the end of the road. His life was in Dublin and it looked like mine was in Galway. But things changed for me again. My mother was beginning to say that she was no longer able to make the journey to Galway to take care of the children when I got sick. Now almost seventy, she felt she'd done her bit. Because I had no family in Galway, I did look forward to the visits from Dublin. My mother was my rock and the primary carer of the children and me when I was taken to hospital.

The children loved to see their Nana coming from Dublin with her bag of goodies. She always managed to pick up a bargain somewhere, whether it was a pair of stockings or a few bars of chocolates. She never came empty handed, and manys a happy Christmas the children and I shared with her in Galway. She'd fuss over the turkey and delight at telling them her stories of when Santa used to come to her. Even though she hated Christmas up to this, I firmly believe the Christmases she spent in

Galway with my children were as treasured as the memories she gave to all of us.

I'd been in hospital a few days now with another respiratory infection. My temperature had subsided and the antibiotics had kicked in. This was just another routine infection. I always found hospitals to be great places when I was sick, but if I was feeling anyway better at all I didn't want to hang around. It was during my stay there that I happened to pick up a copy of the *Galway Advertiser* and somewhere in the public notices I saw an advert for a competition being run by the Hospital Savings Association. They were looking for people to write in to nominate their mothers as the best mother in England, Scotland, Wales, Northern Ireland and the Republic of Ireland. I picked up a pen and began to write. In my letter I told them briefly of my mother's life, how she'd got married and reared us and was now looking after her grandchildren. I wrote that she was always there for us, just like a doting mother hen. She was my rock in times of trouble and she never judged me or turned her back on me. I told them what a wonderful carer she had been, nursing both her sisters through cancer, and now here she was again looking after me when I'd get sick, always taking care of my children when I had to go to hospital. I put the letter in an envelope, addressed it and one of the nurses kindly posted it for me.

A couple of months later, my mother received a letter from the HSA to say her daughter had nominated her as best mother in the Republic of Ireland and, what's more, she'd won. They'd arranged a dinner for all the family at the Hilton Hotel. My mother was in shock. She'd never won a prize before, except a few bob on the bingo, so when she rang me up to ask me what had I done, I couldn't tell if she was angry or happy. She had the newspapers ringing trying to follow up the story, but she didn't like being in the limelight. So I rang them back and told them that she wouldn't be doing an interview as this special occasion was going to be a private one.

My mother had never been anywhere posh before and didn't even know where the Hilton was. There was only one other time in her life when she had a big day out. As a young girl she worked in a jeweller's in town and the boss brought all the staff out for the day in his Bentley. They'd had a relay race in the park and her team had won. She often told us the story when we were young, going over the details of the dress she wore, the smell of leather and the sun glinting off the chrome fittings of the car. And now here she was off to the Hilton, the poshest place in town, wondering what clothes to wear and hoping my da wouldn't get drunk and spoil it for her.

The hotel was magnificent and I know she felt a million dollars that night. I was so proud of her sitting at the top of the table and being awarded her trophy and plaque 'Best Mother in Eire.' She deserved it. She was one of the best, and as for my da, he was on his best behaviour that night. We all had a great time and her plaque still hangs proudly in the sitting room, even though, sadly she herself is no longer with us.

So if she wasn't able to come down to us, and Marty wasn't there to help fill her role, I was really stuck. I paced the floor many nights before I came to my decision. If Mohammed couldn't come to the mountain – then the mountain was going to have to go to Mohammed. So it was with great trepidation that we packed up our belongings in June of 2000 and headed east.

I don't know how I managed when the children were smaller, I thought, as I packed up another box of photos. I was getting sick too often and maybe moving back to Dublin would help establish relationships with the rest of the family. The children would need someone there should anything happen to me, I reasoned. I said a sad farewell to my friends in AIDS West and thanked them for all their support over the years. But I had to do what I thought was right for the children and me.

Marty was delighted at the news that I'd decided to move back to Dublin. He was there to help me pack up everything and he transported our belongings across the country. As I stored all my belongings in my sister's garage, I wondered how long it would be before I saw any of them again. I'd given up my job and my council house in order to start over and I prayed that it would work out for us. I had yet to find accommodation and schools for the children, but Marty promised to help sort everything out with me.

At first we stayed back where I'd grown up in the flats. The corporation refused to house us, sayng I'd made myself homeless by giving up the house I had in Galway. Private rented accommodation looked for vast deposits, a month's rent in advance and references from previous landlords; none of which I had. Social Welfare again also refused to help with a deposit, saying I'd made myself homeless. After four short weeks of living cramped up in the flat with my mam and da, my father came in drunk one night and threw us out.

'I don't care where you go, but you're not staying here. Now get out.'

History was repeating itself. My life had gone full circle. I had gone from working with homeless people to being homeless, and it all happened within a month of leaving Galway. I went to the welfare office in Charles St. on Dublin's northside, a dilapidated old building dealing with the homeless, and told them I had nowhere to go. I was given one night's accommodation in emergency B&B in Mountjoy St. and told to come back in the morning with the docket-slip as proof that I had stayed there.

Arriving at the B&B on Mountjoy St. that night with the three children (Damien was allowed stay at the flat with my parents), I was met by a burly man in his mid-forties.

'Do you have a docket?'

'Yes. Here it is.'

'Right,' he said, as he examined it, 'these are the rules. No drink. No drugs. No visitors. No leaving the kids alone. If you're not in by eleven o'clock, you stay out. And no noise.'

With all those rules it sounded worse than a prison. The street was aptly named.

'What time is breakfast?' I asked in my innocence.

He threw back his head and laughed.

'You must think this is the Ritz, there isn't any.'

Mountjoy St. was very basic. We were given one room with 3 beds, a makeshift wardrobe and a window that looked out onto the street. The toilet and shower were shared with a girl in the next room called Grace. I could tell she was stoned the night I moved in. There was just herself and her three-year-old son Josh across the hall. I saw little of them until the night she knocked on my door.

'Hey, Anna. Do you mind if I look out your window?'

I didn't get to answer as she sailed past.

'It's just I'm expecting company.'

Pulling back the curtain she looked out onto the street.

'He's there alright. Listen I'm going to bring a friend up, but don't answer the landing door if anyone knocks, OK?'

'It's nothing got to do with me, Grace, what you do; just don't involve me in whatever you're up to.'

I could hear her run down the stairs. Seconds later I heard voices and a door closing. A couple of minutes after she'd closed the door, someone started banging on it.

'Grace, open this door now. I know you're after bringing some fella in there.'

The key turned in the landing door. There was more banging from the burly man downstairs.

'You're out of here, Grace, if you don't open this door now.'

The door opened and out ran Grace's friend.

'I know you had him in there, using.'

'I didn't. I swear to God I was only showing him something.'

'If that child wasn't asleep I'd throw you out this minute. I'll be back in the morning. Remember I'm keeping an eye on you.'

The next morning she was asked to leave. When she told him she'd nowhere to go, he told her he didn't care; he was giving her five minutes to get out. I couldn't stand living in this environment and every morning we got up early and walked the streets. There were times when Mam would have a bit of dinner ready for us, but I knew she was up against it with the ol' fella and there was only so much she could do. So we'd call down to Focus Point in Temple Bar and get a cheap dinner. Sometimes we'd even have enough for dessert. And I thanked God for Sr. Stanislaus and her spaghetti bolognese.

I was now officially on the homeless list of Dublin Corporation. What had I done? Left behind my lovely house, my job, neighbours, my support system, to walk the streets day after day with nowhere to go. I had taken my children from a warm secure home to this. I had made the decision to come back so that I would have support if I got sick, and here I was in a worse position than ever. I was now caught between the devil and the deep blue sea.

After a number of visits to Charles St. with my docket slip they told me they were moving me to another emergency accommodation. This time I didn't have to bring the docket slip back anymore. My new residence was again a single room on the top floor of an old building on the North Circular Road. Up four flights of stairs, this room had a set of bunk-beds and a double bed with a street-facing window that didn't open. On my landing were two other families. Between them they had six children. We all had to share one toilet and one shower. On the floor below, three more families lived in similar conditions. The ground floor was called the sitting room and kitchen, but these were rarely, if ever, used. When it rained, it poured in from the extractor and down the cooker onto the floor. Generally it looked like the rats were more at home down there than anyone else. This emergency accommodation, I was told, had its own caretaker who was employed by the landlord to supervise the running of the building. She lived across the road and oversaw any comings and goings from the building. No drugs, No drink, No visitors. They were the rules.

My first encounter with the caretaker wasn't a good one. It was almost midnight when I heard the loud banging on my room. As soon as I opened it, she started her rant.

'Some child is after spilling paint all over the sitting-room floor. So you all have to get up and come down and clean it. There's a corporation inspection in the morning and if the place isn't clean, they'll close us down and you'll all be put on the streets.'

'Look, that's not my problem.' I said to her. 'My children are in bed and we don't ever use the sitting-room.'

'I'm after calling everyone in this building to go down and clean the paint, you included.'

'Well I'm telling you, I'm not going down to clean up a mess my children didn't make. You're the caretaker, you deal with it and don't come banging down my door again at this hour; my children are asleep.'

'So you're not going to clean it?'

'No, I'm not.'

'Right so, hand over your keys. You're out of here first thing in the morning.'

'You can't put me out.'

'Yes I can. Now give me the keys.'

As I handed over the keys, I realised the high price of opening my mouth and taking a stand.

Early next morning I picked up the few belongings we had. As I passed the kitchen some of the other residents were still there cleaning it. The atmosphere was hostile, but I could sense their fear as they silently watched me leaving, next time wondering if it would be them. It was seven o'clock in the morning as I boarded the bus to town, three sleepy children in tow, wondering why we were once again on the move. The bus was packed, but we were lucky to find a few seats on the top deck. As we neared the city centre, I watched the young men and women, all neatly dressed, hair gelled and smelling beautifully. Some were listening to walkmans, others chatted on mobile phones, all ready to start their day's work in the offices and shops in town. The Celtic tiger was roaring all around me and I wasn't part of any of it; it had completely passed me by. I wondered how my life had come to this. As I pressed the bell to get off, the bus came to an abrupt stop and four breakfast bowls and spoons went hurdling down the stairs, followed by a half eaten box of cornflakes. All around me people sat staring. Oh God, the humiliation. Then a young lad in a swanky jacket bent down to pick up my cornflakes. 'Nothing like Kelloggs in the morning,' he said. I thanked him as we stumbled off the bus. There was some decency left in the city where I was born. I was grateful for that.

'Where to now?' I thought. I'd have to call to my mother's first and tell her what had happened. After I told her my story, I went over to the Corporation offices in Fishamble St. I asked to speak to someone in the Homeless Section and I made a report about the caretaker. By teatime that evening the landlord had returned my room key and told me I was welcome to stay as long as I needed. The caretaker was later dismissed from her duties and I returned with the children to the room at the top of the house on the North Circular Road.

CHAPTER 23

It was late summer 2000 and I was finding it increasingly hard to cope. I'd no home, no job and very little money. The children were due to start in their new schools and I was sinking deeper and deeper into depression. The stress of living a homeless life left me with little appetite. The future looked grim and I couldn't see a way out of this homelessness. The City Council continued to say I had put myself in this position by giving up a local authority house, while the welfare system refused to help with a deposit for private rented accommodation. I was stuck in a rut and I couldn't see anyway out. All I saw was darkness and endless misery. When the children had climbed up onto their bunks at night and gone to sleep, I often found myself sitting on the toilet floor out on the landing ringing my hands and quietly crying. They were very dark days and lonely nights. As a result of not eating properly, my weight plummetted and I lost about two stone that summer. At times, I felt weak from malnourishment, suffered bad headaches, fatigue and malaise. I weighed seven and a half stone.

Often during the day if the weather was fine, we'd walk around Stephen's Green or Merrion Square Park just to pass the time. On the wet days we frequented the museums. They're another great place to while away the time when you're homeless. We spent hours in the Natural History Museum, looking at the different stuffed animals. It was dry, it was warm and it cost us nothing to wander around looking at the giant elk or the foxes. The children became quite fond of the stuffed animals. They would have competitions to see who could give them the funniest names. It wasn't my favourite place however, as looking at the stuffed animals in their glass cabinets made me feel as dead as they were.

It was on one such day having done the rounds of the free parks and museums when we were strolling down Grafton St. and I spotted a familiar face in the distant crowd. I stopped dead in my tracks. I thought I was seeing things. It was Simon, dressed in a black t-shirt, Levis and runners. I could hardly mistake him. His hair looked different though; it was longer now and was tied back in a small ponytail. I watched as he went to use the bank machine on the corner.

'Jesus, Mary and Joseph,' I swore out loud. He had a bank card. He had money in a bank. I was completely shocked.

'Mam, what's wrong with you?'

It was Rachel. But I didn't answer.

I followed Simon with my eyes. He wasn't alone. Across the street a young woman with brown curly hair waited for him. She was well dressed and wore a white crochet top and long white skirt. Simon joined her. They held hands and laughing they continued on their way up the street.

'That was your father.'

'Where? Where?' The children's heads starting to turn in every direction, their voices all a panic now.

'He's just walked past you, wearing a black t-shirt.'

'I didn't see him.'

'I didn't see him.'

'I did. He's very big isn't he? Why did he walk past us, Mam?'

'He didn't see us. He has other things on his mind.'

'Who was that woman with him, Mam?' Rachel, forever curious, wanted to know.

'Must be his girlfriend, love.'

All the way back to the tiny room on the N.C.R. the questions continued. Some I answered as truthfully as I could, and some I just didn't know how to answer. It had been nine years since I'd left Dublin and now I was back and homeless. I was HIV positive and Simon still didn't know. I'd had another son that Simon had never even met. Now he'd just walked past me and his three children on a busy Grafton St. How did I feel now? Mixed up? Confused? Yes, but also angry at seeing him looking so well. Green with envy because he looked happy with another woman, and even more angry because he was spending money on her when his kids and I had nothing. There he was living the high life walking down Grafton St., hand in hand with a new love in his life and not a care in the world. I hadn't stopped him, confronted him or shouted at him. No. I watched him in a bewildered state of shock because for the first time in fourteen years I could tell he wasn't stoned. Grafton St. really was a wonderland that day.

Seeing Simon again blew the head off me. I began to wonder about his life. What had changed to make him turn it around like that? The hardened heroin addict and well-known criminal had changed. He'd finally done it. Then I remembered all the years I'd sat and listened to the promises that he could never keep and wondered how such a change could have come about now? As I thought about all that had gone before and what I had just seen, my thinking began to change. After years of keeping the children away from him, I now began to wonder if maybe they would be better off being with him; that maybe he could give them what I couldn't, a roof over their heads, a safe bed at night, food and clothes that they needed. I was feeling hopeless as a mother and stupid at having made the mistake of returning to Dublin and ending up homeless. My family had all got on with their lives, bought houses and got better jobs. I felt I hardly knew any of them anymore since I'd been away too long. Dublin had changed almost beyond recognition. The skyline had changed with its chain of cranes to be seen everywhere I looked; there was an ever-rising number of apartments flying up all over the place, endless rows of cars stuck in traffic that brought with it pollution and noise. People were rushing in every direction like ants that had their nest overturned. The Celtic Tiger was alive and kicking. But I longed to be back in the country. Back to the tiny village where we'd first lived, back to the peace and quiet. I wished I could turn back the clock to a time when we were feeding Smarties to the sheep and listening to the birds singing. But I couldn't. Those fond memories were in the distant past now. All around I could hear digging, cars blowing their horns, children crying and ambulance sirens screaming through the traffic. I wasn't coping at all, everything was becoming too much for me and at times I felt I was on the verge of a nervous breakdown.

It was late one evening when I knocked on Celia's door. It wasn't something I'd planned to do, but I was desperate and couldn't think of anywhere else to go. I waited patiently outside with the children, hoping someone would open it soon before I ran away. Eventually, Frank, her husband, answered.

'O my God, Celia, look who's here.'

Celia came to the door, took one look at me and started crying. 'I've prayed to Padre Pio every night to look after you.'

Celia and I were never really close, but on this occasion I welcomed her arms as they stretched out wide to embrace me.

'Come in for God's sake. Frank, what are you doing leaving the girl at the door for? Put the kettle on.'

As she looked behind, she saw the children. 'Is this them?'

'It's three of them. Damien's down in his Nana's.'

'God almighty. Look at the size of them now. Do you know I used to go into the Grotto in Meath St. every Saturday to light a candle, to ask God to send you and the children back to me. Sit down there now. Frank will make the tea. What has you back in Dublin? I heard you were in the country somewhere.'

'We were. We were in Galway.'

'And why did you come back?'

'It's a bit of a long story.' I was reluctant to open up my can of worms just then.

'So you had the baby. Is this him?'

'Yes, that's Gareth.'

'Fine child, God bless him. They all are. Here, open the biscuits Frank and give some to the kids.'

Celia hadn't changed, a bit more grey maybe, but still as bossy as ever. She'd raised eleven children herself with Frank. I had to remind myself that she was Simon's mother, my children's grandmother, though I had never seen her in that light.

'Frank, will you take the children into the sitting-room so I can have a chat with Anna. They can watch a bit of telly.'

'Right so. Come on, gang. Let's see what's on the box.'

'I'm delighted to see you and the children, Anna. I'm glad you came up to see me. But what has you back? Everything's OK, isn't it?'

'Well, no, not really. We've nowhere to live.'

'You mean you're homeless. How did that happen? What about your mammy's place?'

'My mam does whatever she can, but the flat's too small for all of us. I'm staying in emergency accommodation on the northside, but it's just a room.'

'Do you want me to ring Simon and get him to come over? I'm sure he wouldn't want you and the children living like that.'

'No, Celia, I don't want to see him.'

'He's doing really well, you know, Anna. He's been in Coolmine over a year now. Off the drugs this long time. Has a job and his own van and all.'

'Yeh, well for him, while I walk the streets with the children, day after day.'

I was cross with myself that I couldn't stop the resentment from spitting out.

'Anna, let me ring him. It doesn't have to be this way.'

'No, Celia, I have to go. Don't tell him I was up.'

'I won't if you don't want me to, but here take this, it's his phone number.'

As she hugged and kissed us all goodbye, Frank came out to wave us off.

'Don't leave it this long before you call up again. You're always welcome.'

Looking back at the corner, I saw the two figures still standing at the doorstep. In my hand I gripped the tiny piece of paper. 'Throw it away Anna. Throw it away,' I kept thinking but as I crossed the bridge I stuffed the phone number in the back pocket of my jeans. Maybe someday I'll ring him, but not now.

CHAPTER 24

Ever since we'd moved into that room on the N.C.R. there were people coming and going, in and out of the building at all hours. I never minded any of them, as they never really bothered me, and I kept myself pretty much to myself. I got on well with Tina and Ritchie across the hall. I felt a bit sorry for them sometimes, as they were only a young couple and one of their babies had just gone into care. They weren't coping very well either, so every so often I'd mind their baby Jessica just so they could go out for a few hours. Karen, one of the residents underneath, was OK too. She was a single parent with a lovely four-year-old son. They were waiting to be housed.

As it happened, I was in the building alone one night with the children. Everyone else had gone out or hadn't come back yet for the evening when I heard the shouting followed by the landing door downstairs being kicked in.

'Where the fuck is she? The stupid bitch. She's gone and legged it, hasn't she?'

I ran into my room and locked the door. What the hell did they want? They must be looking for one of them downstairs, over drugs or something. Crash went the landing door.

'If there's anyone up there, come out now or the doors are getting kicked in.'

I knew they meant business so I opened the door very slowly. Two large young men stood there.

'Does Tanya Duffy live here?'

'There's no one by that name here.'

'She fuckin' does live here. Dark-haired one. She owes us money.'

'There was a girl with dark hair who lived downstairs but she's gone a couple of months now.'

'You're fuckin' lying.'

'I'm not.'

There must have been something in my voice that made them believe me.

'If I find out you're lying, I'll be back. Do ya know who we are? Well, you will soon enough if we don't find that bitch. She owes us money.'

'Honest, I don't know anything about her other than that she's not here.'

'Right, if she comes back tell her we're after her.'

They turned and headed back down the stairs, shouting at each other as they went. I was shaking all over. It took some time before my heart stopped racing and I was able to breathe again. Gang warfare was something I wasn't getting involved in. Another crazy night followed shortly after that, when four teenage yobbos broke into the house and thrashed the downstairs. Pulling down the fire extinguishers they sprayed it all over the walls and the mouldy carpet. The place was an absolute mess. That was the last straw, I just couldn't take much more of it. Living like this was affecting every part of me. It was also having its effect on the children. They often cried at night too and in the mornings didn't want to go to school. Because I wasn't able to cook in that nightmare of a house, we lived on chips and there were only so many chips we could eat or sausage rolls for that matter which we had on Saturdays. Saturday morning had become sausage roll morning. Often I didn't eat at all now and found myself existing on Colgate toothpaste and cigarettes. I knew that wasn't good for my immune system but I didn't have any appetite and the fight was gone out of me. Sometimes I'd ask God why he didn't just take me … take me out of this miserable life … out of this 'Hell on Earth.' Day after day, I was being eaten by guilt at taking the children away from a happy home and away from their friends. I tried to reason with myself that I had done the right thing in coming back to

Dublin. There was no HIV specialist care team in Galway at that time and sometime soon I'd have to consider starting treatment. I'd needed to be near to my clinic in Beaumont but this seemed irrelevant now. I was sorry I'd uprooted the children and even more sorry for the way they had to live. Moving back had been a big mistake.

CHAPTER 25

The ragged piece of paper in my hand was slightly torn. I could barely make the numbers out. I'd put it in so many places, half wishing to lose it, half not. It had been weeks now since Celia had given it to me. It was late and the children were fast asleep as I sat on the toilet floor. It had become a regular place for me to sit late at night; somewhere that the children couldn't hear me cry. I picked up my mobile and dialled the number.

'Simon?'

'Yeh, who's this?'

'Don't you remember me?'

In the background I could hear a screech of brakes and a girl's voice saying, 'Who is it?'

I wanted to hang up when I heard it.

'Anna, Anna, is that you?'

'Yes, it's me. I'm sorry to ring you so late.'

'Is everything OK? Are the kids OK? Where did ya get this number?'

'Celia gave it to me some time ago. I didn't want to ring you but …'

'What's the problem? Where are you?'

'I'm back in Dublin with the kids and we're homeless.'

I had come to this.

'Jaysus, Anna. Don't tell me that you're ringin' me up to tell me you and the kids are sleepin' in some doorway. Tell me where you are. I'm coming to get you.'

'No, look, we're not sleeping in a doorway. I'm in a room on the northside. I'm just ringing to say I can't cope anymore.'

'Do you need money for food or anything?'

'No, I don't want money.'

'You don't sound the best. Will you meet me tomorrow somewhere?'

In the background I again heard screeching, the banging of a car door and Simon shouting, 'Fuck off you. I'm talkin' to the mother of me kids.'

'Yeh. I'll meet you tomorrow evening in Celia's. Is that OK?'

I was still wondering what was going on at the other end of the phone.

'Sure. Will you have any of the kids with you?'

'Probably.'

'Are you goin' to be alright?'

'I'll be fine.'

Nine years. It had been nine whole years since Simon had seen any of the children, though they had seen him that once when he'd passed us in Grafton St. and he hadn't spotted us. We were strangers that day and now we were all going to meet. He didn't even know Gareth had been born all those years ago. Didn't know if it was a boy or a girl I'd had. I'd never told him on my visits to Mountjoy Prison. I'd also never told him I was HIV positive. I'd never felt there was a need for him to know. I'd kept it from him, pretending to him and the world that I had made it. I'd overcome a lot in my life, but HIV is something you can't overcome. It's something you have to learn to live with, and right now I wasn't living at all. My life had almost come full circle. I had gone from working with homeless people to being homeless in a year. I'd encountered the same bureaucracy and red tape as those I had worked with. When you haven't got a proper address, you're a nobody. I'd experienced the same social exclusion, except for me it was a double-edged sword: I was homeless and also HIV positive. I felt cast out from society with a virus I could not talk about. There was no one there to listen. Even amongst those who are socially excluded and marginalised, it is hard to tell those who you share a toilet with that you're HIV positive. You simply don't for fear of repercussions and even more exclusion so you keep it to yourself. I was living an overburdened life in a silent world where I had no voice.

I was a nobody.

I told the children the next day about my phone call to their father. They were surprised at first and very apprehensive about meeting him, they barely remembered him and of course he was a stranger to Gareth. They were also a little bit curious. Walking up to Celia's that evening, I hoped I was doing the right thing. I wasn't sure what it was I was looking for, but I knew a large part of me wanted to hand over the responsibility of the children's care. I knew I was feeling vulnerable, but I was also aware that I didn't want to get bush-whacked into getting back with Simon. I was going to make this clear from the start.

When we got to the house, Celia was there with other members of the family, waiting for our arrival. I was early, and Simon wasn't there.

'Good to see you again, Anna. Come in and get a cup of tea. Simon rang. He'll be here in a few minutes. He wasn't very happy about me giving you his number. He said I should have told him you were up first with me before I gave it to you.'

'Look, if he doesn't want to see me, I'll go.'

'Don't be stupid. Course he wants to see you. Think he's just a bit nervous. It's been a long time.'

'I know.'

'Sit yourselves down. Hey kids, any minute now you'll see your daddy drive up in his white van.'

The children looked from one to the other. Daddy. It wasn't a word they were used to hearing, and one of them had never had an opportunity to say it, so they were very confused as they sat and waited. Then just like she'd said, minutes later, a small white van drove into the *cul-de-sac*. The doorbell rang and Celia answered the door.

In Simon walked, larger than life with his 'Steven Segal' ponytail.

'Say hello to your Daddy, kids.'

Celia still knew how to put her foot in it. I cringed. I could see Simon was holding his breath.

'How are yis? It's good to see yis.'

He couldn't take his eyes off Gareth, and, looking to me, he said, 'And who's this?'

'Gareth, this is Gareth. This is Alan, and Rachel. Damien couldn't come.'

Mumbled voices of hello came from the sofa.

'Right, well, I'm just in from work so I'll have a little wash, change these clothes and then I'll be with ya.'

He was only gone a few minutes when the smell of deodorant overpowered the house. Down he came all fresh and squeaky clean.

'Anna, can I talk to you outside in the van for a while? Celia'll mind the kids.'

Stepping into the van, I knew there were a million questions waiting to be answered.

'So,' he said, gripping the steering wheel, 'what has ya back? And where have ya been?'

'We've been living in Galway. We're back a while now but can't get anywhere decent to stay.'

'You don't know how hard that was for me in there. Have you any idea what it was like meeting you and the kids after all this time? How long are you gone? What, ten years, and you just turn up outta the blue and introduce me to a child I don't know. I don't know any of them kids, Anna.'

'I know, but that's your fault, not mine. You chose the drugs over me and the kids, and I couldn't live like that anymore.'

'If you're here to get back with me, you can forget it. I'm going out with a nice girl now who loves me. She'd never run off and leave me like you did.'

'I'm not here, Simon, to get back with you.'

'What has you back then?'

'There's something I have to tell you.'

'I don't like the sound of this.'

There was silence.

'Well, come on out with it.'

'I'm HIV positive.'

'Jaysus.'

Simon sat and stared out the van window. Moments later and still not able to look at me, he asked, 'And what about the kids? Do any of them have it?'

'No, they're all negative.'

'When did you find out?'

'December 1991.'

'And you're only telling me now. You mean to say you could've died and been buried and I wouldn't have known?'

'Look, I'm telling you now because I can't deal with all this stress anymore.'

'Well, I don't have it anymore. The doctors said I lost it. My bloods are clean.'

'Will you ever stop fucking lying to yourself, Simon? You're only trying to fool yourself, that's all. You're in denial. You tested positive in 1986, and somewhere between 1986 and 1991, you passed it onto me. Simon, I haven't come here to blame you. We were young and we didn't understand.'

'I can't handle this, Anna. You're blowing the head off me here.'

'Maybe I should go?'

'No, stay a couple more minutes, then I'll drop you back to wherever you want to go.'

'We're staying in emergency accommodation. It's just a room.'

'So you're in a hostel with a load of junkies and weirdos. You know, I had a feeling you were going to tell me something bad. So what happens now?'

'I'm not on any treatment, but I might have to start sometime in the near future.'

'I can't fuckin' believe this. I'm in Coolmine in my second year off drugs. The lads out there are great. They really helped me get me head together. I was in a bad way after you left, nearly OD'ed a couple of times. It's gonna take a lot to get me head round this tonight.'

'I better go get the kids and we'll head back to our room.'

I went into the house gathered up my family and said goodbye to Celia and her sisters. Climbing into the back of the van, the children sat quietly.

'So what sort of music do ya like? God, they're very quiet. Are they always like this?'

'Destiny's Child,' Rachael piped up.

'I don't think I have any of them. I'll try to get some for the next time. That's if your ma lets me see yis again.'

Darting a glance in my direction he looked for my response but I didn't answer. He started up the van and moved off. When we got to the flat on the NCR, he asked, 'Can I give you a ring tomorrow? I work in the day and go back in the evenings to Coolmine.'

'OK, so.'

Simon did call the next day, and every other day after that. If he didn't get me on the phone, he'd sit and wait outside that house on the NCR. Gina, the girl who loved him, was pushed to the wayside. I was sorry about that, she didn't deserve it. He offered to rent a house for me and the children, but I didn't want to be under an obligation to him or be pushed further down the list to be housed. I'm sure that also would have meant him moving in and I didn't want that either. He got a new car, as he thought it didn't look right for a whole pile of kids to be getting out of the back of the van. This time, he said, he wanted to do things right, and no amount of talking to him could convince him that I didn't want us to get back together. 'It didn't work last time, and it's not going to work now,' I told him.

'But it's different now. I'm off the drugs. I have a job and a car and all I want is my family back. I want to be able to provide for you and the kids like I should've done years ago. I want to make it up to you, Anna.'

Tempting words if I could believe them.

The millennium year was coming to a close; the forecasts had been wrong about a global collapse, though my own world had crumbled around me. It was now early December 2000. Simon's family had arranged a night out for the girls and he felt it was an opportunity for me to meet up with them all again. I, on the other hand, was very unsure even though he'd been very supportive recently when I'd had a tooth extracted and had to be stitched once again. He brought the children food to eat; made sure I got plenty of rest and checked in on me regularly to see if I was OK. I could see he did have his good points despite everything we'd been through, and so it was with good intentions that I agreed to go. Simon wasn't going to be there anyway. It was a girls' night out. I'd also mentioned in passing during one of our many conversations that I didn't like men with ponytails. It reminded me of the Miami Vice era, men in shiny suits and ponytails. I didn't know he'd take what I'd said on board, so I was surprised when he turned up to drop me at the girls' party, sporting a new tight haircut.

'What happened to you?'

'Thought I could do with a change. A change is as good as a rest, isn't that what they say? Do you like it?'

'Yeh, suits you better short.'

And it did.

'You look lovely. The girls are all dying to see you. Are you ready?'

'Just have to get a jacket.'

'I'll drop you there and then you can ring me when you want to be collected.'

When we got to the pub where we were to meet, Simon did something I thought unusual at the time. He parked the car and in we went, said hello to all his relations and then he went for a walk around the pub before he left again. I thought it strange but said nothing. Celia and the other aunts and sisters were all pleased to see me. There was great chat and laughter, but as the night went on, I got more and more tired. Soon all I was fit for was to go home.

'I think I'll make a move now, Celia.'

'What? But you can't go yet. Simon's waiting on you to ring him.'

'I'm a big girl now, Celia. I'm well able to make my own way home. I'll get a taxi. It's no problem. It's late and all I want is my bed.'

'And what am I going to tell him when he asks me where you are?'

'That I'm gone home and I'll talk to him tomorrow.'

The taxi dropped me to my door and I was very glad to get into bed. It seemed my head had barely hit the pillow when I fell into a deep sleep. I awoke to hear the hall door getting kicked and out on the street someone was shouting my name. It was Simon. I picked up the phone. There were ten missed calls.

'Oh, Jesus, what does he want now? Can he not just go home and let me sleep?'

Still groggy from sleep I went down the stairs. As soon as I opened the door, Simon grabbed me by the throat and smashed my head against the glass door.

'Why did you fuck off and leave me? You fucked off and wouldn't answer your phone.' Smack, he hit me across the head with his own mobile. 'What's the point in me having a phone if you don't ring me?'

'Get your hands off me. All I wanted to do was go to bed. I got tired. I don't need to explain myself to you.' His hand lashed out again. This time it was my face and I slumped to the ground.

'You don't love me. If you loved me, you wouldn't hurt me.' I knew my pleading sounded very limp.

'Get in the car. Get in the fuckin' car.'

'I'm not going anywhere with you. Leave me alone.'

He picked me up and dragged me kicking and screaming over to the car. A passer-by intervened.

'What's going on here? Leave her alone.'

That was a big mistake on the stranger's part. Simon lashed out at him and boxed him in the face. The man ran off as fast as his legs would carry him. With me locked inside the car he drove erratically around the corner. The car screeched to a halt. As it stopped, I pulled the button on the door and kicking it open, tried to make a run for it. Grabbing me again, he flung me across the car. Just as he did, two garda cars pulled in alongside us.

'A report has just come in that a woman was being assaulted.'

Simon was quick to reply.

'No, we're just having a bit of a discussion, officer. That's me wife.'

The garda turned and looked at me.

'Would you like to make a statement against this man?'

I couldn't believe it. Here were the gardaí standing there, asking me if I wanted to make a statement while my abuser was sitting beside me.

'No, it's OK.'

How stupid can you get? Did they really think I could make a statement while he was beside me? Could they not see that my life wouldn't be worth peanuts if I did that.

'Well, if you're sure, we'll be on our way.'

They drove off.

'Anna, get in the car now. I can't believe you fucked off on me tonight. I thought you were gone again. You don't know what that does to me when you just disappear like that. I'm sorry for fuckin' hittin' you, Anna, but you make me so fuckin' mad. I'm tryin' to deal with you comin' back with the kids. To top it all, you tell me you have AIDS and that I gave it to you. Do you know what that's like for me? Knowing that me bird is going to die because I gave her some poxy virus. I've been telling meself for years I don't fuckin' have it, and you sail back into my life and tell me you do. I've been living in denial, Anna. No one knows I have this, only you.'

Then there was silence. The penny had dropped. He didn't want anyone to know he had this virus, and he certainly didn't want anyone to know he'd given it to me.

'Denial is a river in Egypt,' he said. 'And I've been living in it for years.'

My body ached all over. I had bruises everywhere. My face was black and blue. I was an absolute mess. I wondered how stupid I'd look if I wore sunglasses in December but really I didn't care. I didn't care about anything anymore. I should have been able to see that hiding coming when Simon walked into the pub where I was to meet the girls. He was checking the place out before he left, to see if there were any potential young men that might chat me up, and when I wasn't there when he came to pick me up, his possessive streak exploded. For all the outward changes, the clothes, the job, the absence of drugs, there was still the violent possessive personality inside.

My mother had always said a leopard never changes his spots. She was right. He hadn't changed. When was I going to accept that I'd made the wrong decision getting back in touch with him? Drugs may no longer have been a part of his life, but he was still the same angry man prone to violent outbursts. Even though he said he loved me, I also felt there was a part of him that really hated me. A part that despised me for walking out on him all those years ago, a part that never forgave me for returning. The mood swings, the violence, none of that had changed. If anything, I had more to fear than ever now that he had nothing to lose by taking my life. He'd always said he'd do time for me and he was more at home in prison than he was on the outside. He had spent most of his life institutionalised; killing me would be easy for him, I thought. I was in a state. I had to get away. Pulling on the sunglasses, I stared out of the crummy room on the NCR watching the busy street below. Anxious motorists sat in traffic beeping their horns. For a moment, I envied them and their impatience. Beeping because they were a little delayed on life's journey. At least they had somewhere to go and knew where they were going. I picked up the phone and dialled Marty's number.

'I need to see you. I have to get away.'

'What's after happening?'

'I'll explain when I see you.'

'OK, where?'

'As far away from town as possible.'

'The Square in Tallaght at lunchtime then.'

'Thanks, Marty.'

I hadn't spoken to Marty for some time now, and had never told Simon about my relationship with him. At least I had enough sense not to do that. I have no doubt but that it would have put both of our lives in danger, and I was in enough trouble as it was. I gathered up the three children and told them we were going shopping. We all got on the No 77 bus to the Square. When we got to the other end, Marty was there to meet us.

'Anna, what's this about?'

'It's about this.' I turned towards him and he saw the bruises.

'Jesus,' he said under his breath as he searched in his pocket and took out some money.

'Kids, take this and go on in and have a look around the shops. Get yourselves something to eat. Me and your ma's just going for a coffee, OK.'

'Cool, thanks, Marty,' they all chimed and, delighted with themselves, they headed off into the shopping centre. We went to the coffee shop and the waitress brought us two coffees.

'Anna, take off the glasses.'

I did as he asked.

'Jesus Christ, look at the state of you. Look what he's done to you. That fuckin' bastard, I'm going to kill him.'

'Marty, he doesn't know anything about you, about us. I never told him you even existed for my own sake as well as yours. God knows what he'd do if he found out. How am I going to get out of this?'

'Well, you can't stay here; that's for certain. Look at you. Jesus!'

As I stared into the coffee cup, I wondered how yet again my life had gone so wrong. How could I have been so foolish? Was I ever going to learn the lessons that life was throwing at me? Was I never going to be able to get him out of my system? Not, I thought, until he got me, or this virus got one of us. I didn't know about him, but I was going to keep on fighting to the end. Marty was saying something to me but I didn't hear him as I was distracted by someone calling my name above his voice. I lifted my head to see where it was coming from, my eyes making contact with a woman I hadn't seen in a very long time. It only took a second for her name to register. It was Angela, an old friend I had known from schooldays.

'My God, Anna. What happened to your face?'

'It's a bit of a long story.'

I introduced Marty to Angela.

'Pleased to meet you, Marty. It's that Simon fella, isn't it? He's done this to you?'

'Yes, I foolishly resumed contact with him again.'

'Some contact that, after all the time you've been gone. I called to your house you know, years ago, to invite you to my wedding. He answered the door and told me you were gone and you weren't coming back. Then he slammed the door in my face.'

'I never knew that.'

But how could I since I thought I was gone for good; never thought I'd be coming back either.

'I just don't know what to do anymore,' I continued. 'I'm back living in Dublin in this grotty dump. I can't get a house and I've him on my case on top of everything.'

'He could always be a right bastard, Anna, couldn't he?'

'Yeh, I've just been so stupid for getting myself into this mess.'

'You should be able to live in Dublin and not have to keep running away from him. You don't have to put up with him beating you up either.'

I knew Angela was right.

'If I could only get my hands on him, it'd give me the greatest pleasure to break his neck,' Marty said. I could tell how upset and angry he was.

'You just don't get it, Marty, do you? What am I supposed to do? Report him? Get him charged? Get a barring order? It's not worth the paper it's written on. A barring order is not going to keep him away from me. What do I do, wave it at him when he breaks into my house?'

'There must be something you can do? I know what I'd love to do with him.'

'Ah, Marty, I know you mean well, but you haven't a clue.' Angela looked from one to the other of us. 'Seriously, Marty, you seem like a nice bloke to me, but have you any idea what he'd do to her if he seen the two of you sitting here together? What he'd do to you? I'm going to tell you something now. The best thing you could do is get out of Anna's life and stay out of it, because you're only putting her life and yours in danger.'

I could see Marty was shocked by her words. I turned to look at her. She hadn't changed a bit. Life had been good to her. She still had her long dark hair and blue eyes that sparkled. She wore little make-up. She didn't need anything to hide behind, for when she spoke, everyone listened. That was Angela, never afraid to speak her mind.

'I know you think I'm joking, but it's no laugh. I'm only thinking of what's best for you and Marty in this mess. Now, what are we going to do? I think you should get the kids together and come and stay with me for a while. What do you think, Marty?'

'Well, she doesn't have any other choice, does she? Going back is out of the question.'

'Right, that's sorted. You get the kids. The car's outside. I'll ring the husband, tell him I'm on my way.'

'What about Damien?' Marty asked.

'He's not with me.'

'Where is he?'

'He's in Nana's.'

'Ring him. Tell him we'll collect him on the way.'

'On the way where?'

'To Meath. I live in Co. Meath.'

And that was how my next escape came about. I stayed with Angela and her family in Co. Meath for two days. It was Christmas again and she found room at the inn for the four children and me. Then she hired out a mini bus and drove the children and me back to Galway to a refuge. Angela was in her last year in college, studying to be a social worker, something I had great dreams about doing myself all those years ago. I've no doubt she made it. She showed all the signs of making a great one and we would have been one hell of a case study for her if she ever needed it.

CHAPTER 28

Christmas is the busiest time of year for women's aid refuges. It's also the saddest for the women and children who find themselves having to spend their time there. A time when the world at large is singing about peace and goodwill and every mother wants to bring a sense of magic into the lives of her children. This is what I wanted for them too, so I made the best I could of it by putting up a small tree in our room in the refuge and wrapping gifts for them. Little gifts I picked up for them, here and there, in pound shops and second-hand charity shops. I could tell they weren't happy being back in the refuge again, especially Damien. He didn't stay long with me. He was fifteen, a young man who was fed up with his mother moving all over the country. He took a stand and said he was never leaving Dublin again, except for a holiday. I understood. He returned to his Nana and I made the best of what was left of Christmas in refuge, but on New Year's Eve, I headed east and returned to that grotty little room at the top of the house on the North Circular Road. Marty met the children and me at the bus stop.

'Good to see you again, Anna. You made it over Christmas?'

'I did.'

'I have some Christmas presents here for you and the children.'

'You know you didn't have to do that.'

'But I wanted to.'

His kindness made me cry inside, but he was edgy and kept looking over his shoulder.

'What's wrong with you?'

'You know, Anna, you're the only person I've ever gone to meet with a bag full of Christmas presents and a hammer.'

'A hammer?'

'Yea. Just in case the other fella turns up. If he does I want to wish him a happy Christmas as well.'

Leaving Marty in O'Connell St., I wished him a happy new year and headed back to the house on NCR. Little did I know how my new year was going to begin. In the early hours of the morning I got a message from Simon telling me to come to the hospital as fast as I could, as something had happened to Damien. Simon met me at the doorway of St. James' Hospital.

'What happened?'

'Me ma rang me. He's after getting a bottle in the head.'

'This is your fault. Where is he? If anything happens to my son, I'll kill ya myself. Get out of my way.'

I rushed down the corridor and searched frantically for Damien in the A & E. I prayed he'd be OK. I remembered that other time vividly when he was only weeks old and I was praying then that he would pull through. There had been a lot of drama in my life since then I thought, as I continued to search for my fine strong son. I found him lying on a hospital trolley, his head and neck covered in blood.

'Damien, it's me, your mother. Are you OK?'

He stirred and tried to look at me. Blood was drying black and crusty on his cheeks.

'Nurse, he's going to be OK, isn't he?'

'He'll need some stitches but I'm sure he'll be fine. I'm just going to clean him up a bit.'

'Damien, what happened?'

'I was walking down the road with a couple of the lads and their girlfriends, and this gang was passing us on the path. There was a scuffle and one of the other fellas threw a bottle, it hit me in the head.'

'Jesus. Let me look at you.'

'Ma, I'm alright, stop fussing.'

Outside, Simon stood, his head hung low.

'I'm sorry, Anna.'

'What exactly are you sorry for this time, Simon?'

'Everything. I really am. I'm sorry I hurt you and made you go away. I was just so angry because you left the party and didn't wait for me to collect you. I know I'm such a fool. But, you know, I'll never stop loving you, Anna. You mean the world to me. You are my world. You are my life.'

I saw Marty once briefly after that New Year's Eve. We met for coffee. I knew any relationship I had with him was well and truly over, but I hoped maybe we could remain friends. So when my mobile rang and it was Simon saying he had the two boys in the back of the car and he was parked outside the vegetable shop, just doors down from the coffee shop I was in, I knew it was time to get out of there, quickly. A harmless cup of coffee with someone whom I once lived with really wasn't worth the risk of Simon's rage. Harmless as it was, I knew there'd be no explaining it to Simon. So for both our sakes, I crept out of the coffee shop and crossed the road, pretending to come from the opposite direction altogether, allowing for Marty to make the last exit out of my life.

'Where were you in the name of God? These two are starving. I got off work early and picked them up from school.'

'I was just out having a look around the shops.'

'Still no sign of that house you're after?'

'No, no news. Hope something turns up soon.'

'Well, you won't accept my offer of renting you a house. How much longer is this going to go on? I'm in the last phase of the treatment programme now with Coolmine. I'm living out there with them other three fellas and I never get to see you.'

That wasn't exactly true. While Simon was looking forward to graduating from the treatment programme and was living with three single working men, he was always parked somewhere in Dublin waiting to pick me up. In fact it became a regular joke between us. When Simon boasted once that no matter where I was in Dublin he'd find me within five minutes, my reply was 'you must think this thing's a helicopter.'

Simon's graduation from the drug treatment programme had taken him two years. He had spent more than half his life on drugs; I knew this was a major achievement for him and I wouldn't have missed it for anything. He graduated along with six other young men. Each had members of their family there for the special day. Tears came to my eyes when Simon's name was called to receive his certificate and some of the lads roared 'Speech, speech.' I looked through the crowd at Simon. He'd made it.

'Well, I'd like to thank the staff of Coolmine for helping me to get me life back together, to the lads for the support along the way and to Anna and the kids for coming back into my life.'

There was a big round of applause followed by cheers. Simon came through the crowd and kissed me on the head. 'I did it.'

He did and despite everything I was proud of him. He had kicked the habit and had the certificate to prove it. Full of his achievement, he said, 'let's celebrate, let's go away together!'

'Away where?'

'Down the country, you, me and the kids. We'll rent a house or mobile or something.'

And that's what we did. We rented a house for five days near Killarney, Co Kerry. Our first holiday together, ever. The house was at the foot of the mountains, miles away from anywhere. It was a very old-fashioned farmhouse. Simon fussed about, keeping the house clean. How he laughed with delight when he saw a cow in the back garden. He organised trips for the kids to see Fungi, the dolphin, in Dingle and brought them swimming to the Aquadome in Tralee. We enjoyed every minute of our trip to Kerry, our visit to the fairy shop in Killarney and our tour of the lakes. Simon's favourite photo of himself was taken beside a sign that read, 'Beware – car thieves operate in this area.' We laughed the whole time in Kerry and I have great memories of the time we spent together there. It took us away from the harshness of the reality of living in Dublin again. It gave us a chance to be in the countryside near farm animals, and away from the stress and the strain.

It was in late October 2001 when someone in the housing department rang with the offer of a small two bed house in Crumlin. At first, I was uncertain because of its size. But it was a house and I accepted. Moving in was easy. I had nothing to move so that solved that problem. For months I'd been telling Simon not to be rushing things. He said after four kids, I was a bit late telling him that and anyway we'd a lot of time to make up for.

'Time,' he said, 'is something neither of us has much of.'

So with the quick purchase of a set of bunk beds and a loan of some camp beds, we all moved into the tiny house in Crumlin. Time was something, I was to learn, which was very important to Simon. His life had become so regimented from living in Coolmine. What time he got up. What time he ate. What time he came home from work. What time he went to bed. And whatever time we spent together after that was never enough.

I started to feel unwell again. I developed a rash that itched like crazy and started to cause me countless sleepless nights. Despite visits to the hospital and various types of steroid cream, no one had a name for the condition and nothing would get rid of it. Simon was freaked. 'What if you die before me? Leave me with all the kids. If you go, I'll be gone the next day. I couldn't live with myself if anything happened to you.'

'Will you stop thinking morbid? We have our whole life to live.'

'Yeh, but that's it you see, we don't. One of us is going to go before the other.'

'Will you stop talking like that? Of course one of us is going to go before the other.'

'But I want to be with you until we're old and grey.'

'If you don't stop talking like that I'll be grey by the end of the week and you won't have long to wait then.'

'I know. I just worry, that's all.'

The walls took on the colour of the tea that had just been thrown over them.

'Tea-stained walls. Maybe we can start a new trend in décor.' said Rachel. 'I'm sick of you and him always arguing.'

'I know, love, I know. If its not one thing, it's another.'

What were the chances of me growing old and grey now. The pattern continued, the rows, the violence, then the apologies, the trying to make up for it. Somewhere up on the bedroom wall written in pencil when we first moved into the house was a date 14th February 2003, the date we set to get married. The day would not come now. I'd never marry him. On the bedroom floor lay the blood from another vicious assault the night before. Of course he always gave humble apologies afterwards and sometimes even cried. The struggle. The torment. The doctor stitched me up again and told me I'd soft tissue damage to the head. As a result, I'd get headaches and nose bleeds without any warnings. Maybe the next time he got me would be the last, so I made a plan. I was now very experienced in the art of escaping. I had it down to a T. So in April 2002, I left Crumlin and again went into a safe house to take refuge with the children. This time I went to Wexford. I posted back the keys of the house to Crumlin together with a letter telling the corporation I was no longer requiring the house, as I couldn't live in it due to domestic violence. I rang the ESB and the gas company and had all services disconnected. I lived in a hostel for a few weeks in Wexford. It was safe and very clean and the people that staffed it were very helpful and kind. Eventually, I rented a cheap house that needed a lot of repair in a good area in Wexford. The landlord had bad tenants before me and was kind and gave me some paint to fix the place up a bit. I didn't mind the physical work; it was therapy for a short time and gave me something to do while I waited to find some work. I got the children into schools, took on two cleaning jobs that didn't pay an awful lot, so I worked in the kitchen of a pub as well. With three jobs I had no time to socialise, even if I wanted to, and vowed to get on with my life. I had no friends in Wexford and no time to make any.

Two months later, I got a phone call.

'I know where you are, and I'm coming to get you.'

It was Simon.

'You're bluffing.'

'You're in Wexford. I know 'cause I found out through the bank where you're making your withdrawals.'

'If you come anywhere near me, I'm going to have you arrested. Do you hear me?'

'I'm on the road to Wexford and I should be there in an hour. And I'm going to kill you.'

Barely able to dial the number my hands were shaking so much, I rang the garda station, the first time and only time I ever rang the gardaí.

'Please send a garda up to my house,' I pleaded.

Within minutes a garda car arrived at the house and after years of abuse, I gave my first statement of complaint. I told them I was living in fear of my life and that the danger I was in was very real. They told me they would put a twenty-four hour watch on the house and together with the women's refuge, the alarm would be raised if the landing curtain was pulled down off the window. It meant I was in trouble and couldn't get to a phone. The gardaí were both understanding and vigilant and even said they'd watch out for a car of that description nearing the town.

As it happened, Simon never made it to Wexford. An ambulance man rang me to say he'd crashed the car and was being taken to hospital. I rang the guards to inform them and later they confirmed he had indeed crashed the car around the Arklow area and had been taken to hospital with minor injuries.

The statement I made was passed over to Simon's local garda station in Dublin who all knew him so well. He was called into the station to answer some questions regarding the complaint. Simon knew the guard who was dealing with the case, so it ended up that he was able to read the complaint himself, even down to my name and address on the top of it.

In fact, the whole episode became even more unbelievable when the guard himself rang me up to tell me he remembered me from years ago and would I not go for couples counselling as Simon was so heartbroken without me? And sure wasn't he great giving up the drugs after all those years? He told me he was an ex-alcoholic himself and sure counselling could do wonders for people.

After the shock of what he said, I asked him did it not matter that he threatened to kill me?

'Ah sure he didn't mean it. We all say things we don't mean.'

'Well you know what they say, if you want to know a person come and live with them. You might think he's Mr Wonderful, but he's a street angel and a house devil.'

This would be the first, the last and the only time I ever made a complaint against Simon. I just said 'what's the point', he knows where I am and he'll find me somehow wherever I go, so I might as well just give up.

CHAPTER 29

Unlike Dublin and Galway, Wexford had no support services for people affected by HIV/AIDS, so when Beaumont started ringing me and asking me to come back for more tests, I knew something was up. I was told it was fairly serious, my viral load had increased, my T-cells had dropped dramatically and I had also come back with a Hepatitis C positive result from the lab. It is hard to say when I became infected with Hep C, as for a long time I tested negative. I went from a negative to positive result and back again several times until finally it was determined that I was Hep C positive. My body was under severe strain. It was time to start treatment. I had been on a pentamidine nebuliser as a preventative measure for P.C.P. for some time, as I was allergic to Septrin which would normally be the first line of treatment, but my cell count was showing that my body was struggling.

As yet, I'd still never been on any anti-viral treatment and the thoughts of it terrified me. Simon and I had both known people over the years who had gone on treatment and were dead in months. Of course treatments were much more advanced than they used to be, but I still felt they were toxic, came with side effects and the longer I stayed away from them the better. In regard to Hep C, it did come as a surprise that I had it, but then Simon had that too. It seemed the lesser of the two evils, and since I reckoned I coped well with HIV, I could cope with Hep C. I did ring AIDS West for support and decided I would go back to the hospital, but I wasn't ready to start treatment. I wanted to forget all my worries and go on holiday.

Simon had moved back in with his mother Celia, and after the episode he came down to Wexford every weekend to see me. He never hit me again. I booked a holiday to the Costa del Sol and the six of us went away for a week in the sun. Apart from England, Simon had never been away before, so this was a brand new experience for him. When you're strung out on gear you're not thinking of holidays abroad, you're thinking of where you're next fix is coming from. Since that was now in the past he could think of other things. I was beginning to notice that his health was also starting to suffer. He had never acknowledged his HIV diagnosis to anyone but me and now it was really taking its toll on him. I noticed how tired he was all the time. Mornings were best for him, and he enjoyed getting up as the sun rose and going alone for walks along the beach. He told me he'd seen a beautiful sand sculpture of a mermaid on one of the walks and it really gave him great peace of mind. He had little energy now, had lost weight, didn't have an appetite and his skin had turned very sallow. We had talked about starting treatments and he said that stuff was not for him, but that he'd support me in whatever decision I made regarding my own treatment and, after all, he believed the hospital knew best.

In the afternoons he'd have to lie down to rest so he could make it out in the evenings. I brought him to a karaoke bar on the last night of our holiday. I told him I'd put my name up to sing. He laughed and said I hadn't the guts, so when my name was called, he couldn't believe it, and as I got up on the stage, he went to the back of the pub to see my only performance ever of Patsy Cline's *Crazy*. The crowd clapped and cheered as I made my way back to my seat. Sitting down I looked at Simon; there were tears in his eyes. 'I'm so proud of you.' Another of the few special moments in our messed up lives.

Back in Wexford, Simon spent most of his weekends sleeping. We did have another good day out at Johntown's Castle and together we talked and walked around the grounds and lake. I admired the beautiful peacocks with their colourful feathers. He said that they were just birds that liked to show off and his favourite bird was a magpie.

'Why a magpie?'

'Cause they like to steal shiny things and they're always up to mischief. When I die, I'm going to come back as a magpie and follow you wherever you go.'

'Is it not bad enough that you haunted me in this life without haunting me in the next one?'

We both laughed and held hands, and when we got back to the house, he fell asleep again. He was very dependent on me and never wanted me out of his sight. The first thing he did when he woke was to call my name. He even did it when I wasn't there, he told me. He didn't want to be alone.

CHAPTER 30

In October 2002, I packed my bags. I was sick and losing weight rapidly. The rash was still there. It hadn't gone away. My eyes were in the back of my head for the want of a good night's sleep, as every night I'd wake up scratching and I'd cry because I was so tired. I'd been to different doctors and I'd heard every type of diagnosis from psoriasis to different types of allergies. I was even told by one doctor (bless his cotton socks) that I was allergic to the new Euro currency. This I found hilarious, as I never had any money to be allergic to.

It wasn't until the hospital did a biopsy that I was told the only way to stop the disease progressing and the virus from further weakening my immune system was to start treatment. And the sooner I did this the better. I couldn't do this living in Wexford with no support. I knew Simon was sick too. I couldn't look after myself and him and the children. This time I wasn't leaving because of drugs or any violence; I was leaving to get the medical help I needed. I left Simon a letter telling him I hoped he'd do the same and change his mind about starting treatment. For me, I knew I had no choice now. In the letter I told him I'd forgiven him for all the bad things he'd done and that I loved him and would always love him.

With the help of support services I again went back to Galway and this time rented a house in the city. My health was failing and I knew this time it was serious. I prayed the damage done to my immune system could somehow be reversed. On December 12th, almost eleven years to the day I was first diagnosed, I began treatment. My T cell count had plummeted to sixteen and my viral load was up in the hundreds of thousands. Triple therapy antiviral treatment was to be a routine I had to stick to if there was to be any hope. It consisted of Combivir, Neviripine and Dapsone, all to be taken twice a day. I felt sick and tired, hungry and full and my insides felt upside down. I had twice-weekly hospital visits to Beaumont to watch for side effects, and any signs of my condition worsening. Even those double journeys to Dublin from Galway took most of my energy, energy that I couldn't afford to waste but I couldn't see any other way. Beaumont was monitoring my health as there were no such facilities in Galway at that time. Things have changed since. Galway now has its own Infectious Disease Clinic and people can avail of the services there instead of travelling over two hundred miles round trip to get counts checked.

I posted Simon a Christmas card from Beaumont hospital on one of my visits and sent it to Celia's address. On the front was the poem 'Footprints.' I had told Simon about the verse some months back; it was my way of telling him we had to have hope. Inside, I wrote 'Happy Christmas and a great New Year, love Anna & the kids xxxx.'

On Stephen's night, I rang his mobile. 'Hello, Simon. How are you?'

'Ah, Anna howiya? The kids, how's the kids?'

'I've been better Simon, I'm not great. The kids are fine. How are you?'

'I'm not the best myself, but fuck it.'

'Are you alright? Are you drunk or on drugs or something?'

'No I'm not, I'm sitting here watching the Simpsons.'

'OK then, look after yourself, and I'll talk to you soon. Happy Christmas, Simon.'

'Happy Christmas, Anna.'

That was strange. He didn't sound himself. No giving out, no rows, no cursing down the phone.

A special hospital visit had been made for me to attend on Jan 2nd, so I planned to visit my friend Al and stay in my mam's flat the night before. When I called to Al's, she was delighted to see me as always. We sat there chatting and drinking cups of tea, but as the night went on I began to feel worse, and finally I told her it was time for me to leave. With a lot of pain and discomfort I arrived back at my mother's flat and settled on the sofa. My head hurt and I was finding it hard to breathe. I felt as if the life was draining from my body. Twice during the night I called my mother to tell her I needed to get to the hospital. She wanted to call an ambulance, but I didn't want a fuss. I thought the morning would never come, and at first light I set off for Beaumont Hospital. The doctor took one look at me and told me I was being admitted. I knew I was bad but I wasn't prepared for that. I had no nightclothes or toothbrush, but when I rang my mother she told me not to worry about those little things, that I was in good hands now. The time I spent there went by in a bit of a blur. Days turned to nights, and I spent most of the time sleeping. I had lots of visitors, but wasn't up to conversation. I was aware of a neighbour's young daughter, Jessica, in the bed opposite and I asked her not to let Simon or his family know I was there, as I needed to rest. She understood.

It was 12th January 2003, around eight o'clock in the evening when Jessica walked into the ward after one of her home visits.

'Hi Anna. How are you feeling now?'

'I'm OK, getting there.'

'Was anyone up to visit you this evening?'

'Yeh, Mam and Dad are just gone.'

'Was Damien up? Or anyone else?'

'No, why? What's going on?'

I watched her nervously fidgeting.

'No, I was just wondering if you had any visits, or if you heard anything.'

'Heard anything like what, Jessica?'

'I heard some bad news, Anna.'

'What bad news?'

'It's about Simon.'

'What about him?'

'I heard he's dead, Anna.'

'No, he's not. Who told you that?'

'It's all over the flats.'

'No. No. No,' I screamed. 'It's not true. It can't be true. It can't be true.'

'That's why I was asking if Damien was up. Do you want me to ring for you?'

I handed her the phone.

'It's not true, love, it must be someone else.'

'His phone's off, Anna.'

Quickly I took the phone off her and dialled the house number. One of Simon's sisters answered.

'This is Anna.' In the background I could hear people crying and sobbing. 'Tell me this is not true.'

'I can't talk to you, Anna. Damien's here, I'll put him on the phone.'

'Damien, where's your Da?'

'Ma, me Da's dead.'

'No, no, he can't be dead.'

'He is Ma, he was found dead at lunchtime in Tricia's flat.'

Celia took the phone.

'It's true. My lovely son is dead. He died of a broken heart.'

'Please don't do this to me. Tell me he's not dead.'

'The family tried to get in contact with you. Where are you?'

'I'm sick. I'm in Beaumont Hospital.'

'Do you want us to come over?'

'No, I don't want to see anybody,' I sobbed.

'We'll come over in the morning to see you.'

I put down the phone. I wanted someone to tell me it was all a bad dream. I picked up the phone again.

'Hello Al. It's Anna. I want to know if you've heard the news?'

'What news? What's wrong?'

'It's Simon, he's dead.'

'I don't believe you.'

'I don't want to believe it myself. Jessica just walked in and told me he's dead. I've just rang the house. It's true Al.'

I couldn't control my sobbing.

'Anna, I'm on my way over. I'll be there as fast as I can.'

Bewildered, I walked up and down the corridors of the hospital, sobbing my heart out. A nurse appeared from somewhere and made me tea. Al came shortly after and together we sat and drank tea all through the night. I didn't know what had happened to Simon. All I knew he was gone and despite all the violence in our years together, it felt like half of me was missing. The nurse gave me something to help me sleep. It didn't work.

Next morning, I sat on the bed looking out the window of Beaumont Hospital. My thoughts drifted over the rooftops of Dublin city when suddenly a magpie flew onto the ledge of the window. I couldn't believe my eyes, and rubbing them I climbed out of the bed and went over to check. Yes, it was real alright. Sitting all alone was a magpie. He didn't move, just sat there for a minute or two and I cried ... and cried ... and cried.

'The obstacles of your past can become the
gateways to new beginnings.'

(Anon)

When I look back on my life now, it seems that all of what
happened, happened to someone else and not me. How I
got through it all, I'll never know. Instinct, the will to
survive and the love I have for my children have given me
the strength to overcome the obstacles on this life's
journey.

When heroin flooded the streets of Dublin in the early
1980s, it attracted the vulnerable youth from dis-
advantaged areas of the inner city, many hoping for an
escape from the problems they had: lack of education,
unemployment, alcoholism and the poverty that
surrounded them. Some came from loving homes and
others from broken ones. Heroin was the 'Pied Piper' that
called many youth of that generation from these areas, led
them to a life of crime to feed their habits and left them in
that big black pit that few escaped from. Most of them are
now dead. My story is an account of someone growing up
in inner city Dublin and meeting a young man that
followed the 'Pied Piper'. His need and cravings for drugs
led him into a dark world and a downhill spiral and long
lost days in Mountjoy Prison.

With the discovery of a new virus that was causing
deaths amongst the gay community in the USA, HIV soon
began to leave its mark on the world. Little was known
about the virus at that time except that it led to AIDS and,
more often than not, death. The heroin epidemic of the
1980s in inner city Dublin that captured the most
vulnerable from our society in turn opened the door to a

deadly disease with a little name. Ignorance was rife. It was a death sentence that transcended the boundaries of age, gender, sexual preference, race or culture. There were no education programmes, no treatments and no cure. Some saw AIDS as an act of God to rid the world of 'undesirables' ... the sinners, promiscuous people that led immoral lives. In Dublin city, the older generation watched as their sons and daughters succumbed to a life of drugs, sickness and eventual death, leaving them to rear lost grandchildren. Heroin and HIV destroyed families and robbed them of the next generation. Older members that had grown up in tenement Dublin looked on AIDS as the 'new TB'. They remembered loved ones they had lost in years gone by. AIDS to them was just another sickness and one not to be shunned. To that generation, I salute you for having the understanding many others lacked.

My relationship with Simon was indeed a turbulent one. They say opposites attract. In my life I know now that I have made many mistakes and sometimes the wrong decisions, but then I am human. I am not infallible. Although, surrounded by drugs growing up, I never felt the lure. The 'Pied Piper' may have been playing his tune but I didn't listen. I didn't follow in his footsteps. Instead, I followed my heart. It took me on a roller coaster that was to be my life with Simon. Leaving him took great courage. No woman wants to leave a home and take her children into refuge. Sometimes there is no choice. When home is where the hurt is, you have to leave it to seek help.

Simon is four years gone now. I hope to a better life, one where his demons don't chase him and he's at peace. His death was very painful and traumatic for me. His loss is still felt. It's 2007, sixteen years since I tested positive for HIV and 5 since I started triple combination therapy. I'm doing well. My viral load is less than 50 which means the virus is undetectable, even though it's still there, and my CD4 count is between 200–300, a far cry from when it was a count of merely 16 and my viral load was in the hundreds of thousands. I now live back in Dublin with my grown up children. I love them dearly and they're very good to me. I recently celebrated my fortieth birthday at a party with family and friends. An old pal had a special request on the night, *Paper Roses,* and we sang it together just like old times. My eldest son, Damien presented me with a beautiful bouquet of flowers. He will be twenty-three this year and is manager of a security firm. My daughter Rachel is twenty-one and assistant manager in a leading department store. Both are in long-term stable relationships. Alan is now eighteen and off to college soon where he hopes to qualify as a gym instructor. Gareth is soon to do his Leaving Cert. Damien was having a joke with his brother Alan the other day; they were talking about growing up and having nothing.

'Remember when I saw that lovely jumper, Alan?'

'Yeh! And Mam told you to keep your eye off it because you wouldn't be getting it.'

'What was it she always said, Alan? As long as we have each other we'll be OK.'

The room filled with laughter. It was good to hear. Some say laughter is the best medicine. I agree. I'm not bitter at contracting HIV. Bitterness and anger eat away at your soul. I don't blame Simon for my being positive. Simon's denial of the virus and me feeling immune to it were all contributing factors. We were young, naive and stupid. HIV was something that happened to other people, it couldn't happen to me. I know I wasn't alone in thinking that. But HIV doesn't stop to ask questions. It knows no boundaries. That's why I believe education is the key.

In all the times I've been sick and my immune system low, I've learned you have to have hope. Without hope you have nothing. Hope was the special gift given to me by my children the night I sat telling them with grapes that I had a virus. Hope was in the moment when my young daughter took her cough medicine from the fridge and, with her wise words, announced that someday there would be a medicine to make me better. Medical therapies have come a long way in that time. What was a death sentence when I was diagnosed (where people were dying more from the drug regimens than the virus) is no longer the case. People are living into old age due to the combination therapies developed in the last years. I have developed my own combination therapy of conventional medicine, laughter and peace; this has worked for me.

To those of you reading my story who are just newly diagnosed, don't give up believing. For me it hasn't been an easy road to walk but I count myself blessed. Each day that I wake up is a great day to be alive and I take from it whatever joy it brings. When problems stare me in the face I deal with them as practically as I can. I am after all just another mother trying to raise her children in the best way she knows. We all want what's best for our children. I hope in reading this book it has given you an awareness of HIV and AIDS, an insight into growing up in inner city Dublin, its drug culture of the 1980s, and the problems attached to homelessness, life inside refuges and on the run. For those who are living with HIV and the families that are affected by it, remember you are not alone. There is light at the end of the tunnel. Above all have hope.